ENTREPRENEUR: FROM ZERO TO HERO
How To Be A
Blockbuster Entrepreneur

Charles Banfe

*Department of Industrial Engineering
and Engineering Management
Stanford University*

VNR VAN NOSTRAND REINHOLD
New York

Copyright © 1991 by Van Nostrand Reinhold

Library of Congress Catalog Card Number 90-20479
ISBN 0-442-23961-0

Manufactured in the United States of America

Published by Van Nostrand Reinhold
115 Fifth Avenue
New York, New York 10003

Chapman and Hall
2-6 Boundary Row
London, SE1 8HN

Thomas Nelson Australia
102 Dodds Street
South Melbourne 3205
Victoria, Australia

Nelson Canada
1120 Birchmount Road
Scarborough, Ontario M1K 5G4, Canada

16 15 14 13 12 11 10 9 8 7 6 5 4 3 2

Library of Congress Cataloging-in-Publication Data

Banfe, Charles.
    Entrepreneur : from zero to hero / Charles Banfe.
        p.   cm.
    ISBN 0-422-23961-0
    1. Success in business.   2. Entrepreneurship.   I. Title.
    HF5386.B2294   1991
    658.4'21--dc20   90-20479
                                                      CIP

CONTENTS

PREFACE

Vilfredo Pareto was a highly respected Italian economist and sociologist born in Paris about a century ago. He developed the Pareto Principle in which he suggested that most events in life fall into an 80/20 relationship.

Applying this theorem to the business environment, it holds that executives spend 20% of their time on 80% of the problems. That seems reasonable for many executives say they accomplish most of their important decision making in the first hour or two of the day, and spend the balance of the day on least important issues. On the income side, 20% of markets accounts for 80% of a product's total revenue.

This seems to be a fair statement, according to many marketers. They often find that firms derive the major income from small market segments. These small markets take care of breakeven costs permitting them to enter markets which do not provide large sales volumes.

It is also true that when a market share reaches 80% or more, it behaves like a monopoly, with barriers to entry, ability to set prices, and control of distribution.

Applying the Pareto Principle to the study of entrepreneurship, it supports our contention that there are no absolutes; no 100% statements; ambiguity prevails. Eighty percent is more often the case and can be taken as a "truth." That squares with our notion anyway. Malthus said that though we approach truth, we never reach it. Archimedes wrote that there is no pure truth.

Given that fact, we can accept that paradoxes may exist. There will be statements made about entrepreneurship and then appear in conflict later. That is only because, using the Pareto Principle, 80% right is being treated as a "truth" and, in fact, the statement will behave as a "truth." It further acknowledges that every "truth" may be refuted in the minority but that ambiguity does not invalidate the premise.

Let us consider the relationship and motivating force of accomplishment and money in entrepreneurship. Samuel Johnson once proclaimed to a group of salesmen in ancient England, "We are not here to sell a parcel of boilers and vats, but the potentiality of growing rich beyond the dreams of avarice."

Sorry, Sam, but we are not here to talk about growing rich. That is not the objective of this book. It was written as a resource and stimulant for the success-oriented entrepreneur and that does not mean money. Do not be misled. There is no intention to knock coinage of the realm. That red hot mama, Sophie Tucker, was on target when she said:

> "I've been rich, and I've been poor. Believe me, rich
> is better."

It is true that the "potentiality of growing rich" is everywhere in entrepreneurship but only to those who strive for excellence, not to those who chase money alone. Entrepreneurship will not succeed if the pursuit is for money alone. For the motivated, remember:

> Entrepreneurship must be the pursuit of personal
> achievement.

More complicated than merely "selling a parcel of boilers and vats," entrepreneurship is wedged in three complex elements—the strategy, pursuit, and capture.

For example, if an entrepreneur is to succeed, he/she must first have a strategy, a plan. There is a homily worth noting, "If we do not know where we are going, any road will take us there."

Therefore it is necessary to develop a strategic vision in a written form. Though Steve Jobs did not in the formation of Apple and $40+ million, it does not violate the basis thesis. Lou Doctor founded Raster Technologies. When the venture capitalist firm, Venrock, asked him for a business plan, he asked, "What is that?" He was funded for $2.5-million without one.

Yet, talk with venture capitalists and almost to the person, they will not consider a startup without a fully documented business plan. They get one or two business plans each day, spend about 30 to 45 minutes on each one, funding about 1 or 2%. Most successful venture capitalists are so strung out that they will not read a business plan unless it is recommended by a colleague. (That is 80% correct, not 100%, but not bad.)

Incidentally, Sam Johnson might have added that "rich beyond dreams" will happen too, only if the pursuit and capture is made enjoyable. That breezy, irreverent entrepreneur and corporate emir, Sam Zell, loosely runs his $2.5 billion empire. "My motto is simple. If it ain't fun, don't do it." He rides a motorcycle to work even on bone-chilling winter mornings.

Keep Zell in mind throughout the entire reading and you will understand why entrepreneurship can be enjoyable and pleasurable!

Next, the entrepreneur must also be willing to cope with the humiliation of blatant goofs as a part and parcel of startup life. A fundamental lesson an entrepreneur learns is that it is all right to screw up! It comes with the territory. Give a thought to the turtle. The only time he gets anywhere is when he sticks his neck out. To trip or fall flat a few times is not all bad. It may provide valuable learning for the next go around. Those who stumble often refer to it as a step on the staircase to success. They get up, brush themselves off, and move on into the future.

Mistakes are part of the pursuit. An entrepreneur must be able to take/stop losses on goofs and ride with the good outcomes.

Charles J. Givens has created a $100-million fortune teaching life-achievement attitudes. "I've made every mistake with money a person can possibly make," he says. He has lost two fortunes.

Adam Osborne has flatly declared that he was not unhappy with the thunderous debacle of the Osborne computer. "It comes with the turf." He estimates that entrepreneurs have to fail 3.8 times before they succeed. Nolan Bushnell of the staggering Atari, the bombed Pizza Time Theater, the tripped Androbot, is abuzz with Axlon, his current computerized dolls, and has dismissed past failures.

It is worth noting that one roaring successful venture does not ensure a failsafe future. Many entrepreneurs have hit paydirt with one startup and fallen splat on the next one. Failure lurks in every corner, every niche.

Stuart Karl, 32-year old president of Karl Lorimar Home Video, Inc. in Irvine, California, cautions that, as a matter of fact, one success may be less contributing to a future venture than the lessons learned from a failure. But do not give up, Karl urges. Winston Churchill said,

"Never, never, never, never give up!"

There is no set method of learning for the aspiring entrepreneur. Here are some of the ways:

1. Being involved in a startup. This can provide a valuable learning experience.
2. Jumping in. Just plain getting your feet wet is a most common course. With no experience and no knowledge of how to do it, there are entrepreneurs who just plunge ahead. Many new venturers have said that if they had known what was ahead of them, they would never have had the courage to take the first step.
3. Continuing education. Today more than 500 colleges offer accredited courses for the entrepreneur. Over 200 colleges and schools offer full programs in entrepreneurship and more are being added every year. These are a kind of piggyback experience and often given an entrepreneur the confidence and inspiration needed.
4. Working for a venture capital firm or an entrepreneur. Jim Treybig went to work for a venture capital firm to gain experience and then launched his very successful Tandem Corporation.
5. Working for a corporation and intrapreneuring. Frequently, entrepreneurs gain experience by working on a firm's attempt at intrapreneuring.
6. Developing products which are company castoffs. Those who work for large corporations sometimes take products and fill market niches which are unsuited for the corporation but are ideal for a startup.
7. Grabbing rollers of opportunities. Opportunities have a wavelike characteristic. They emerge from obscurity, swell to a crest, and then pass out of sight. They must be grabbed at the first sign. George Gilder wrote in The Spirit of Enterprise, "Once an opportunity is generally known, it is pretty well gone." The sooner the opportunity is identified, the greater the potential for success.

8. Departing a corporation. This can be termination, the inability to hack it with a large company, or just being unable to work for a boss. Don Eldridge worked for Ampex. With a young person over him, Don recognized his chances of advancement were limited. One Friday, he felt he just could not go on. Don (eight children) and four others resigned. They founded a company they called Memorex.

Next, it would seem that there should be detailed pinpointing to sources of material, rather than casual mentions. But the validity of what is referred to would not be enhanced by the "integrity" of the sources because they are so often not in total harmony. Where precise references are relevant, they will appear. Better to look at the underlying logic, understanding that statements are made as the result of the study of many reasonable sources. Conflicting statements exist but are, by and large, minor and can be ignored.

Use this book as a carrot to get on the roll. It is intended to make one think. It is a kind of entrepreneurial haiku—that 17-syllable imagistic and literary form of Japanese poetry. It is a brushstyle inspiration that will hopefully send the blood rushing, and stimulate the creative lobe.

Though the entrepreneur is faced with a vast number of ways to get going, he/she must get going! Getting started is half the battle. Yogi Berra might have said, "If you wanna do business, you gotta do business." Vacillation and indecision are safe, nonthreatening, but unacceptable.

Whatever the excuse for not doing it, one must take the bold first step. Jerry Burgdoerfer, Berkey Photo entrepreneur, said, "I think, if you are stuck in a rut today, it's because you got comfortable there."

The vast majority of entrepreneur ventures are based on derivatives and present technology. The success of completely new technological products is rare. In this book, I do not claim to present a way to become a successful entrepreneur but have taken available data and put it together in a format showing how to make it big in a new venture.

I did not use heavy literature from the past for the field is too dynamic. The material came from three valuable sources. (1) From current periodicals, magazines, and other professional material: this provided inspiration and a source for some of the writing. If there is a similarity, it might be so. Where parts of articles were appropriate, they were used to form the basis of the writing. They were not used verbatim for this would not allow the book to flow as it does. Instead, some writings were redone. (2) From

were redone. (2) From classroom networking with graduate and business students: they were either planning to start a new venture or had launched one or more businesses. Their discussions and comments were valuable for they included experience of many kinds. (3) From successful entrepreneurs who frequently came to the classes. Their input was incredibly insightful. Notes were gathered from each of these distinguished guest lecture sessions.

The book is unique for it is written as a startup—from creativity through harvesting. The material is current and easy to read from any starting page. Enjoy!

Charles Banfe

ACKNOWLEDGMENT

My thanks to energetic students and tolerant friends for their help and to my wife for her generous support. Also to my colleagues at Stanford University for their valuable insights and suggestions. They all made it easier. Dan Van Der Weide, my able Teaching Assistant, is a Ph.D. candidate in Electrical Engineering. He has also started two new ventures. His help was remarkable.

INTRODUCTION

During any given time of the year, entrepreneurial activities in the U.S. are dynamic. More than 12,000 new business ventures are started. Nearly 2000 entrepreneurs pocket their first million as they harvest. Almost 12,000 startups fail. That is entrepreneurship; enormous rewards for some and large losses for many.

Though the odds are not good, if you find a way to beat them, you can be wildly successful. Most importantly, it is there for those who are willing to drive ahead! It may not be easy, but it is worth the effort.

The water cooler wisdom which says that entrepreneurship is something you have or do not, a matter of genetics, that old black magic, the occult, available only to a few lucky persons, a mystique, out of reach to most, is dead wrong. Peter Drucker is right when he says that entrepreneurship is nothing more than a discipline and, like a discipline, it can be learned.

That is the matter of this book: to learn how to be an entrepreneur, how to be creative, how to plan, how to execute, how to be successful, how to reach self fulfillment, how to walk away, and, best of all, how to enjoy life as a result of being entrepreneurial. It is a game plan book culled from the experiences of dozens of successful entrepreneurs.

Throughout the book there will be references to three descriptive components that deserve clarification:

1. Entrepreneurship is the total overlying structure.
2. Invention is the concept, design, and development of a product or service.

These fall into three categories:

- UNIQUE. One of a kind. Less than 20% of all startups are first time products, entirely new technology, or never-before services.
- DERIVATIVE. Add on. About 80% of all innovations are adaptations and improvements of existing products or services.
- COPYING. Cloning. Though for a clone, in essence, to be successful, the new product must have a distinct competitive advantage—price, quality, utility, availability, distribution, size, etc.

3. Innovation is the process of change. It is the process from invention to market.

Starting at square one, there is no set formula for entrepreneurial success. That must not be a deterrent or cause for worry. The path to follow is well marked and there are definite tracks one should follow to maximize chances of success.

What the book will do is show how to recognize an opportunity and how to exploit it. By following the guidelines, the chances of going into successful orbit with a startup will be increased by a factor of ten at least.

First, examine two key elements: the controllable and the uncontrollable. Conception and execution are controllable elements.

They are the two compelling factors in the makeup of successful entrepreneurs. Good ideas are a dime a dozen. They are studies of brilliance when put into action correctly. It is knowing the difference that separates the adults from the children.

Knockout success can be achieved in a startup by a well-developed concept, which is the left-hook, and good execution, which is the right cross.

It is almost impossible to deliver a knockout without a proper concept. But it is also not possible to score a knockout without appropriate execution. Each is different, important, and interdependent.

Lest we forget, it is critical to understand that execution is performance, and the greatest idea in the world is worthless unless it is executed properly. On the other hand, to execute without a concept is so random as to be pathetic.

Charles Schwab, entrepreneurial CEO of the nation's largest discount brokerage house supports the idea that, "There's a difference between concept and execution." One without two is like a second best hand in stud poker.

Luck and Timing are uncontrollable elements. Another Charles, Bodenstab of Battery & Tire Warehouse, turned the firm around with the luck and timing of an unusually severe winter a few years ago. "There's an adage I always keep in mind," Bodenstab said. "If you've a choice between brilliance, luck, and timing; take timing first, luck second, and brilliance third. The flip side is, don't ever confuse them and assume something happened because of your own brilliance when it was really a matter of luck or timing."

Successes have been attained by entrepreneurs appearing to be no-ability, laid-back free spirits who seemed to have stumbled onto a new venture unintentionally, tripped over a cache of money for startup, and fell into a waiting market. Luck and timing played pivotal roles. In 80% of cases of successful startups, the entrepreneur had excellent timing with not a clue that timing was involved.

Entrepreneur Jill Rapaport of General Mills reckons that being in the right place at the right time is extremely important. That is luck and timing, but how to determine the "right" place and the "right" time boggles the mind.

There is a serendipity about entrepreneurship which embraces luck and timing. These two elements are also notably enhanced by an entrepreneur's attitude and outlook.

The success-destined entrepreneur can create favorable environments for luck to occur or the timing to be right and greatly increase the probability of the occurrence. Moreover, they are highly intuitive and at the first sign, they are quick to seize an opportunity and run with it.

The key to luck and timing is early warning recognition and implementation. Some have made it big by following the leader.

Repeating other's successes, with the addition of some competitive advantage, is not uncommon.

Think of all the schussboomer startups. Most are variations on a successful theme. After all, that is the strategy and backbone of franchising! Video games, software packages, pizza clones, personal computer tag-a-longs, and a long list of others fit into the shadow startups. Discount houses were introduced in the U.S., and the copies were soon rampant. Federal Express introduced small package overnight service and in a year, mirrored services popped up all over the horizon. Milton Berle made a successful comic career out of copying. Many have asked, "What have the Japanese ever invented?" No one questions their prowess in cloning, copying, adapting, derivatives, and tailgating. Their robust industries have been successfully founded on a little-bit better adaptation of products proven in the marketplace. But then, that has been the prevailing strategy of one of the most powerful corporations in the U.S.—Big Blue, IBM. The Chinese poet, Li Po, said it 4000 years ago, "If you want to find a way up the mountain, seek someone who has taken that road."

The book is for the person who has an unscratchable itch to start a new business. The path to success may not be neat but there are definite rules of the road and directional signs. Those willing to strike out, to learn, to follow, to persevere; will conquer.

The direction to successful entrepreneurship is clear. The many paths are not, for there is not a single, well-traveled path to entrepreneurial success. The book is raisined with examples of every instance to show how it can be done and has been done. It will chronicle and format entrepreneurship from start to finish.

Perseverance is the key, and a willingness to tolerate mistakes is essential.

In 1958, at 36 years of age, a man failed miserably in four retail ventures in New York City. His low-prices and cash-only concept was good. Execution was adequate, but luck was against him and his timing bad for the market was not ready. A few years later, he tried for the fifth time. The first day's sales were a meager $11.06. He persevered and bulldogged ahead. The man just would not give up; each failure was a stepping stone to success. Now luck was with him and the timing was fortuitous. He hit the jackpot, bringing inordinate success to R. H. Macy.

It is just a restatement of the fact that out there in the deep blue yonder are incredible opportunities, stimulation, and satisfaction which are for the taking.

That is entrepreneurship in the buff.

1
WHAT IS AN ENTREPRENEUR?

INTRODUCTION

Economist J. B. Say defined an entrepreneur as one who recombines capital, physical resources, and labor in some new, more innovative way. Carrying that definition further, an entrepreneur does not open another muffin shop. An entrepreneur creates a different way to serve a muffin; delivering it to homes or customers with a special butter or jam, or some other unusual twist which did not exist before. The entrepreneur finds a new way to market muffins, perhaps aroma or ambience or service. One successful software company advertises that it "sells solutions," not software. An entrepreneur is an avid dreamer, day and night; visionary, planner, and the "de-inertia-ing" force behind every new venture. The entrepreneur is ever restless, always on the move; a retro-powered and committed innovator, a creative gofer; constantly scanning every horizon for an opportunity, poking into the future, looking to bring about change, continuously dealing with uncertainty and the unknown; having the ability to make probabilities out of possibilities and molding dissonance into a melodic tune. The entrepreneur operates in high gear, is driven, thrives on staying loose, adjusting, fine tuning, and is an inveterate fiddler who often upsets what is, which is predictably disconcerting to those involved in the project. The master fiddler, Bill Lear, was like that with the incredible Learjet.

All in all, entrepreneurs are mavericks and soloists who have a rough-hewn approach to things and uncompromising determination to do it their way. It sets them apart in sharp contrast, from those reposing snugly in entitled union jobs or who are cushy number-crunching minions in large corporations. There is plenty of sweat, tears, fears, and precious little glamour in entrepreneur war stories. They are all about roll-up-the-sleeves, tighten-the-belt, get-the-job-done sorts of persons whose motivation and capacity for bulldog persistence and toiling should cheer those who lament about the ho-hum American work ethic.

ENTREPRENEURSHIP EXPLAINED

A science, an art, or even a discipline, Entrepreneurship is hardly. It is sweat laboring in the trenches or a shoot-the-works, gut-wrenching roulette spin more than anything else. Entrepreneurship is rethinking conventional paradigms, discarding traditional ways of doing things. The old and proven methods might have applied in the past, but entrepreneurs are possessed with contriving new ways which are better, or they simply create new and improved products. Entrepreneurship has been impishly described as Blind Man's Bluff, Dylan's Folk Wisdom, Life at Fort Fumble, Sandbox Scandals, Roulette Rompers, and as understandable as Andy Wharhol's Pop Art. Not bad. There are rocky uncertainties and roiling inconsistencies, you'd better believe!

Nancy Austin wrote in *Passion For Excellence,*

> "Most innovations are the result of the wrong person
> at the wrong time for the wrong reason."

Often-times it is a wham-bam Hungarian or impetuous hyperkinetic who steamrolls over a market with a cerebral "Rubik's Cube" or, in other cases, a laid-back, shuffling character who backs into a market spectacularly with a dumb "Pet Rock." By the way, when is the time ripe for an entrepreneuring?

Whenever you are ready!

Wait for better times and conditions? No! What will happen next year? Who knows? Listen to economists? Forget it.

Entrepreneurs should pay little heed to street rumors or what economists predict, for the track record of economic gurus is far from First Class, Economy, or any Class. Economic experts are notable for sepulchral crystal balling, and their visions often need trifocals. They all speak out of both sides of the mouth. An old saying goes,

> "Economists are often wrong but never in doubt."

If they were handicappers, we would be broke by the third race. Senator Hollings defines an economist as,

> "Someone who finds something in practice and won-
> ders if it would work in theory."

Some economists are like one of the great scientists of the forties, Vannevar Bush. He warned President Truman in 1945 to forget the atomic bomb,

> "The bomb will never go off and I speak as an expert
> on explosives."

Economic forecasters find a safe haven on the negative side, more likely to be cautious, or to predict a chary four quarters, doom and gloom replete with early warning signals. That position is reputation-insuring. If they are wrong and the year is a banner one, the public does not mind. If Economists hand out glowing statistics for a bountiful year and miss, they are roundly chastised. Their skills are then in question.

Some noted,

> "Economists predicted ten of the last four depres-
> sions."

Think of this. Not long ago, eleven noted economists made predictions in four categories for the coming year. Not one was close! Astrologist Jeanne Dixon was most on-target.

For the same year, a lionized Harvard economist made seven predictions and he bombed seven times! He was wonderfully eloquent and exquisitely urbane in a backlook dissertation of why the economy did not follow the logical pattern he had predicted. His stature as a respected economist was untainted.

Stan Levine once lamented in *Forbes,*

> "Either the economists are too low or the analysts
> are too high."

If the product is ready and a market demand is identified, the time for entrepreneurs to get started is today. They must be true believers of the paradigm,

> There is never a bad time for a good deal.

Just do not rationalize. Do it—today!

The activity of Entrepreneurship is composed of two critical components: invention and innovation. Invention is the idea, concept, creation, brainstorm, or bug in the ear. Someone is thunderstruck with an idea of a product or service and invents. Innovation is the process of change, doing it, putting it through the motions. Innovation rarely evolves as formally planned, but rather out of a chaotic charade of unpredictable happenings.

Joseph Schumpeter was correct when he wrote,

> "Economic progress, in a capitalistic society, means
> turmoil."

Innovation occurs because some hard-driving megalomaniac (or easy-going choirperson), makes it happen. Some persevering persons simply do not know that there are tasks which are impossible. For them, the impossible challenge takes a little longer. About 80% of the successful startups in the United States owe their success to knowing the market and technological development in products, quality, and manufacturing improvements.

Compact cars, VCRs, laptop computers, pocket TV's, tapedecks for joggers, solar energy, CD's, quartz watches they are just a few. Technology has been and will continue to be the primary power to motivate entrepreneurs in our society. Keep in mind that an entrepreneur is one whose product is invented (unique), adapted (derived), or copied (cloned). It succeeds because it possesses a significant competitive edge. The highly respected venture capitalist, Arthur Rock, calls this the "unfair advantage." A 10–20% competitive advantage is a necessary differential. Most are derived or cloned. But it does not matter if the product is unique, derived, or cloned. The result must be value added or a discernible benefit; better product, better price, better distribution, better service, or a better way of satisfying the demand. Entrepreneurs are such a radical breed as to occasionally thumb their noses at such conventional wisdom. They have been known to develop an off the wall product they want, with no regard for the market, and it has zapped the market detractors and become a big hit. The key is that the entrepreneur has a streetsmart market instinct, or is just lucky. It is not the kind of strategic thinking one should adopt. Such shooting-from-the hip has a low success rate, and there have been no repeat performances.

Steve Wozniak invented a personal computer because that is what he wanted to do. The idea was rejected by Atari and Hewlett Packard, dubbed unmarketable. The two Steves, Jobs and Wozniak, stormed ahead. "No" was not in their vocabulary. Only after it hit the stands did Wozniak and Jobs discover the market was ripe for the Apple computer. Woz's most recent invention is a remote LCD switch which he believes is a unique technological breakthrough. He was not sure what it could be used for . . . at the time! Jobs' latest product, the NeXT computer, is derived, an aggregate of present technology, bunched in a creative way to produce an outstanding piece of hardware. Both will probably succeed, for perseverance is their heartsong.

Colonel Harlan Sanders lived in his car for two years peddling and demonstrating a Kentucky Fried Chicken recipe and breaded chicken product. He ate only when he was demonstrating. A persevering entrepreneur in his sixties, he experienced more than 1000 door slams. It should have been a humiliating put down, but he did not know that. He knew only perseverance.

Theodor Geisel (Dr. Seuss) sent his book to publishers and received more than 200 rejections. He persevered and hit a grand slam homer. Gibbon persevered for twenty-six years, writing his *Decline and Fall of the Roman Empire*. It was thirty-six years of perseverance for Noah Webster writing his dictionary. He crossed the Atlantic Ocean twice to gather material.

Cicero practiced speaking before his friends every day for thirty years of perseverance, to perfect his elocution.

They are a few of those who bulldogged, persevered, and did not lose focus or waver. Silicon Valley has been the frontier of high tech entrepreneurship. The San Francisco Peninsula is circled with entrepreneur pairs who started in garages, nurtured, and ended up with multi-million dollar ventures. Steves, Wozniak and Jobs, at Apple, David Packard and Bill Hewlett at HP, Paul Levy and Mike Devlin at Rational, are only a few of the garage duos in point. Garages have spawned myriad new ventures. There is a great deal of useful information that profiles an entrepreneur examples of success and failure, myths and truths to consider, and the paths they followed. For example, entrepreneurs are typically uncomfortable in a holding pattern! They are skittish about inaction. They have the "dithers," that in-motion syndrome. They are leapers! They want to get going—anywhere. They will not be deterred by obstacles. They run roughshod when need be. They know no boundaries. Instead of motion sickness, they despair inactivity and can get inert sickness, a common entrepreneur ailment. Education has a significant place in entrepreneurship, for it will always be a valuable tool. Most entrepreneurs have pursued education in preparation; basic, advanced, or continuing schooling. Successful entrepreneurs have an intelligence base, acquired or acquiring. Most have college diplomas, not all.

It is as Pasteur wrote,

"Chance favors the prepared mind."

Steve Wozniak thought education important enough for him to go back to the University of California (incognito) to finish degree requirements after the Apple triumph. He wanted to sharpen his wits before launching his latest venture, Cloud 9. Focus and motivation are standard equipment and common bright headlights leading through a maze of roads in the black of night. Here is another saying to go by:

The true entrepreneur knows no dead ends, sees only turns in the road ahead.

Moreover, it is often first generation immigrants who are shining examples of entrepreneurship. Massachusetts Governor Michael Dukakis observed,

> "The business leadership in this State is first, second,
> or third-generation immigrant. Just look at a few of
> the names: Wang, de Castro, D'Arbeloff."

TRAITS

Recently, a group of successful entrepreneurs were studied. The following was revealed as to what makes an entrepreneur function. They:

1. Are self starters (typically from an entrepreneurial family).
2. Come from *all* educational levels and environments (from elementary school dropouts to Ph.D.'s).
3. Exploit technological breakthroughs well (that means technological improvement over a current product or development of a new product).
4. Have an uncanny gut feel for the market (new products should have a 10–20% unfair advantage).
5. Have a killer instinct for spotting trends (and acted now, post haste).
6. Are realistic about their skills ("know thyself" was the lapidary advice on the temple of Apollo at Delphi and applies today).
7. Are totally focused and committed (zeroed in on the new venture and dropped everything else, no half-baked endeavors).
8. Cannot work for anyone else (nobody but nobody. Most left because they were terminated, by mutual consent, or simply fed up).
9. Are ladened with motivation to achieve (in a recent study, 80% of successful entrepreneurs queried had achievement as a goal and had not considered money as one of their new venture objectives. Aretha Franklin's song, "Respect" is a song which tells the story, "All I want—is just a little respect. Just a little bit. Sock it to me. Sock it to me . . . " It echoes Rodney Dangerfield's woeful quest for "A little respect.").

COMMON MYTHS

"Entrepreneurs are high rollers." Most entrepreneurs are not high rollers. They do not believe they are high rollers or gamblers. They do not even think they are risk-takers. Entrepreneurs, more often, contend that they are low rollers and risk-averse. It is not that entrepreneurs do not know the value of risk but that their downgrading of risk is a mindset characteristic of entrepreneurs. Risk taking in new ventures is frequently misunderstood. Whatever a new venture is, the outcome is not a certainty, and the uncertainty can be properly defined as managed risk. Nevertheless it is argued that a risk, however stated, is taken. Peter Drucker sees risk taking in a different perspective:

> "Risk taking is what it's all about. We hear a lot of talk about techniques that minimize or even eliminate risk. Nonsense. To try to eliminate risk is not only futile, it can be harmful. The bigger your job, the greater the risks you should be taking. *The idea is not to eliminate risk, but to take the right risks.*"

Entrepreneurs usually view from a different plane. They do not call a new venture risky in the traditional sense for they have identified an exploitable niche and viable product, with the highest probable end result. They loathe to perceive a new venture as risk taking at all, in the conventional sense. Their intuition is so strong and their conviction of what they can accomplish so positive.

Some venture capitalists also use intuitive techniques. Bob Boole and Larry Sullivan of Analog Devices search for young businesses in promising niches in the technology field. Once they find situations that "smell right," they put up both money and expertise. Boole and Sullivan have a highly developed, intuitive senses, and would argue persuasively that it is not gambling at all. It is controlled risk-taking, so controlled as to be negligible. That cultured sense of smell for measuring risk works for them. A customer profile taken at gaming tables in Reno, Las Vegas, and Atlantic City reveals relatively few entrepreneurs in the casinos as opposed to wage earners, who risk their wages and get their high roll kicks in hot pursuit of the big jackpot.

"Entrepreneurs are loners." Studies have shown that most entrepreneurs are married, gregarious, and outgoing. That is not to say that entrepreneurial marriages are smooth sailing, for they are not. Entrepreneurs get caught up in their new venture and everything else sits on the side. Only a tolerant and understanding spouse can deal with playing a minor role to a time-stealing new venture.

"Entrepreneurs are easy going." Not on your life! They rove at a pace as if there is no tomorrow. They are often compulsive and demanding. This abrasive behavior prevails because of conflicting Maslowian needs. The need to achieve dominates while the need to please has been sublimated.

"Entrepreneurs were not always achievers." Studies have shown they were always achievers, even as youngsters. They had newspaper routes, sold lemonade on the corner, mowed lawns, baby sat, and picked up pocket money in many ways. As a child, Peter Ueberroth was an achiever, though his school grades were only average. He went on to develop a multimillion-dollar travel agency in Los Angeles. Then he made an incredible success of the Olympic Games, both financially and societally. Ueberroth went on to become the most successful Baseball Commissioner in the game's history.

He comments,

> "You live in a country where you can do anything you want! A 'C' student in high school, I can go on to become Commissioner of Baseball!"

With an investment group, he recently purchased Hawaiian Air Lines in the Islands.

"Entrepreneurs are only city bred." There is overwhelming evidence that most entrepreneurs are suburban, not inner city, or ghetto raised. Though entrepreneurs of rural communities have not fared as well, they still emerge in large numbers.

"Entrepreneurs are the youngest in the family." Just the opposite. Entrepreneurs are more often the first born. They are, typically, the oldest or an only child.

It may be that the first born is genetically the most talented, then given the most attention. Curiously enough, studies have shown that most entrepreneurs have had strong relationships with their father.

"Random associations are not important." Chance happenings are inextricably woven into the fabric of successful entrepreneurs. Military buddies, neighbor chums, college classmates, childhood pals, work associates, party friends, and club acquaintances often develop into strong business and worthwhile relationships. Former Secretary of the Treasury, William Simon, met a friend on the nineteenth hole at his golf club. It developed into an arbitrage partnership that earned more than $100 million in a few years. Most entrepreneurs point to one person who made the difference and there seemed to have been an unintentional randomness about their meeting.

"Entrepreneurs are erratic." They appear erratic because entrepreneurs usually wear half a dozen hats, bubble with a stock of ideas, are juggling ten opportunity balls in the air, and are trying to accomplish two dozen tasks at one time. Many are not familiar with the Management-By-Objectives (MBO) theory, completing one task at a time. Therefore, it appears that they are not consistent, but the evidence shows that the successful ones have a good sense of tracking priorities and are consistent in solving problems even while appearing flighty, impetuous, and erratic.

UNCOMMON TRUTHS

1. They are totally committed (no partials, no pauses—all the way).
2. They are pin pointed in one direction (A gung ho urgency).
3. They have their goal firmly in mind (Goal sighting is a number one priority).
4. They are leaders (willing to assume leadership and take authority, responsibility, and accountability).
5. They do not ignore details (but are not nitpickers).
6. They learn how to manage time (work smarter, not longer).
7. They have high standards of ethics (all in one boat—self and others).
8. They sincerely like people (nurturing and caring and understanding).
9. They whistle while they work (able to enjoy, otherwise it will fail or not be worth it).
10. They have no idols, but rather, they like performers (no personal biases, performance oriented).

What makes an entrepreneur challenges specific description, for they are moving targets. Any definition is filled with ambiguity, conflict, and paradoxes, often arousing strong feelings and contradicting opinions. Entrepreneurs are not to be thought of in terms of a median or a norm. We see them in the thrall of patterns with wild standard deviations.

There is not a single description of an entrepreneur that covers everyone, just a bunch of characteristics which seem to be common to most. An entrepreneur can only be adjudged in metaphoric and approximate terms, and all myths and truths must be subject to the 80/20 rule. The bottom line is that entrepreneurs are simply made up of people who are shakers and movers, can overcome obstacles, have about half a dozen characteristics which can be learned or, if already possessed, can be enhanced.

2
WHO CAN BECOME AN ENTREPRENEUR?

PROFILE OF AN ENTREPRENEUR

Forget who you are, that you have never started a new venture, and do not have the foggiest notion of how to start one.

Never mind that you do not fit a "typical" entrepreneur mold. Must an entrepreneur fit an "only those who can" mold? No! Never! The evidence is irrefutable: there is no such thing as an absolute profile! Success stories of entrepreneurs fall into outrageous patterns. Successful entrepreneurs abound from every walk of life. You absolutely can become a successful entrepreneur! Being an entrepreneur is less a matter of who you are, what you know about startups, than of what you are willing to do. First and foremost, an entrepreneur is a dreamer. If you can dream, you can be an entrepreneur, no matter who or what!

Here is a solid entrepreneur's paradigm,

> Only a daydreamer can become an entrepreneur.

In Arthur Miller's *Death of a Salesman,* Willy Loman said,

> "A salesman (entrepreneur) is got to dream, boy. It comes with the territory."

How true, Willy. When Willy no longer dreamed, he botched it!

The entrepreneur is a Type A (sometimes B) forager, with a developed intuition and a strong gut feel. Some are spring-loaded, cocky, motivated, positive, focused, optimistic, independent, creative, impatient, intuitive, energetic, with an idiosyncrasy of playfulness. Others are dull, quiet, introspective, reserved, patient, and seem to be better placed at a rolltop desk with a green visor and black arm protectors. But appearance and personality traits do not tell a story, for an entrepreneur is a throwback to the 49'er in the Gold Rush days. He/she is a maverick with a wild imagination, anxious to get started in the uncharted wilderness of startups. No fantasy is too great, no dream too far out, and there is little daylight between dreams.

Flatfooted Charlie Chaplin starred in the silent movie, "Shoulder Arms." Asked how he captured 13 Germans single-handedly, Charlie replied in a simple and mystifying fashion,

> "I surrounded them."

That is pure entrepreneur talk.

In 1924 Tom Watson joined a very small company. They made unromantic products, such as meat slicers and punched-card machines. Tom Watson was a dreamer of the first class. He worked his dream into that company. In his mind, slicers and punched-card machines were only the beginning of the firm's potential. The company grew and grew and grew, into a megacorporation, International Business Machines (IBM)! When Watson was later asked, "At what point did you dream of the company becoming so big?" He replied, "Right at the beginning."

After dreaming a startup dream, entrepreneurs open their eyes and knuckle down to a do-it-yourself reality. In the beginning, the hours are long and the pay, if any, is at poverty levels. What can be more frustrating than not to be paid for hard work done and to have to put out money for the privilege besides? Liz Claiborne is the founder of Liz Claiborne Inc. Her starting advice is,

> "Start with a low overhead and be willing to do everything yourself."

Entrepreneurs start in the shadow of uncertainty, elation, frustration, disappointment, exhileration, playtime, success, and failure. They are mo-

Motivated by the thought of finding a diamond in the rough of a Death of a salesman

tivated by that dream to climb to the top of the mountain. The entrepreneur has to learn to cope with the dimly lit future and a winding, craggy trail. It means picking one's way blindly and stumbling in and out of difficult problems. The progress is torturously slow and often demeaning. But that is par for the course. With all that, the entrepreneur lives by the credo, TGIM,

"Thank Goodness It's Monday!"

In the final analysis, the entrepreneur is held responsible for the success of failure of his or her venture.
Mark Twain said it best,

"The man with a new idea is a crank, until the idea succeeds."

There are two kinds of new venture starters: Entrepreneurs, who are alone, and Intrapreneurs, who are corporation-sponsored entrepreneurs, within the safe confines of a company. The difference between the environments of the Entrepreneur and the Intrapreneur is significant. The Entrepreneur takes all of the gamble and risk alone, while the Intrapreneur takes on a new venture under the protection of a corporation. An Entrepreneur works in the dark, by intuition and gut feel. The creative right brain "hunches" bombard the Entrepreneur while the left brain logic fights back. Gymboree founder, Joan Barnes, reminds the Entrepreneur,

"It's lonely at the top!"

Successful Entrepreneurs learn to use their intuition, described as knowing something without fully comprehending. Entrepreneurial gut feel is an integral byte of intuition, an aggregate of personal experiences, sniffing the vapor of past happenings, and sifting subliminal signals of yesterday and today, applied to tomorrow.
Bob Heller said,

"Never ignore a gut feeling, but never believe it is enough."

When Ted Turner was asked how he knew there was a market for a 24-hour news program, Turner spoke from his gut feel,

"I just knew it."

Intuition and gut feel have always been part of entrepreneurial mythology. If Entrepreneurs rely on their intuition, they can use their instincts to advantage. An Intrapreneur labors under the protecting corporate wing by prescription. That is, nestled in the armpit of committees and approvals. Decisions are a lengthy process. Few who fit into the Intrapreneur socket are willing to handle the uncertainty and insecurity of the Entrepreneurial life. The corporation is a natural choice for those who are conservative, reluctant to depend upon intuition, put their instincts on the line, and not risk takers. They are best rooted as fully vested employees of a Fortune 500 company where they live in combination-lock security by prescription, do not take chances, and are safe in an unrocking boat. There they follow left brain thinking, lemminglike, logical, secure, get regular paychecks with correct deductions, fringe benefits, develop a paunch, and have a predictable future.

Later, they might become Intrapreneurial starters for their corporation but without personal risk.

The Intrapreneur's success is rarely spectacular, but the mishaps are not far either. This does not mean that Intrapreneuring is forever. Some Intrapreneurs work for corporations long enough to gain experience and confidence.

When they have gathered enough experience and confidence, they sever themselves from the parent company and take the giant step toward Entrepreneurship. It is an occasional happening.

But, as Neil Sedaka sings,

"Breaking up is hard to do."

An Intrapreneur *cum* Entrepreneur must be prepared to cut the corporate umbilical cord permanently. It is likely a Point of No Return, for most large organizations have decidedly negative vibes about taking former employees back who have gone out on their own. This is because of a possible rerun scenario at the first new opportunity. Another problem associated with leaving is the labeling as an unstable, restless person. It is a known fact that readjusting to hum-drum corporate life is difficult. There is not likely to be a fallback job waiting.

H. Ross Perot of Dallas, Texas was ensconced in a marketing position with Big Blue, IBM. He discovered a potentially profitable market segment in providing installations and ongoing services for IBM customers. IBM management did not see it his way. They turned him down cold. Not possible. He knew intuitively it was an incredible opportunity.

Perot believed as Tertullian (160–230 AD),

"Credo Quia Impossibile."

The literal translation is,

"I believe because it is impossible."

With $1000, he left a secure job with Big Blue to start Electronic Data Systems (EDS). He was not expecting to return. In so doing, he founded the data processing services industry. His dream reached harvest when General Motors bought EDS for $2.5 billion.

It is evident there are no limitations and anyone can do it. Very clear is the fact there is no set path that successful entrepreneurs follow. Though dreaming, intuition, and experience are all valuable tools, a lack of any one of those is not a defeat in the making.

Who Can Become An Entrepreneur? Anyone Who Wants To

Person

They are tall, short, bald, hairy, fat, thin, muscular, flaccid, athletic, couch potatoes, hyperactive, and plain lazy.

Sandra Kurtzig, founder and President of ASK, was once a frustrated housewife. Steve Jobs followed a guru to India to live for a time. Mike Hollis, founder and President of Air Atlanta, was black and educated while Famous Amos was black and uneducated. The late An Wang, of Wang computers, was a Chinese immigrant. Hispanics, boat people, political refugees, retirees, teenagers, social dropouts, amputees, and paraplegics all started new ventures. Efforts to articulate a profile have failed so badly that little further study has been undertaken.

There is no supportable evidence that successful entrepreneurs fit any person pattern.

Age

Studies have shown the entrepreneurial bell-curve peak to be in the early thirties. Young people have more energy. Thus, there are more young entrepreneurs.

Of the new businesses incorporated a few years ago, more than 65,000 of the 200,000 entrepreneurs were under thirty. Thousands were over sixty! Age has not proven to be a determinant. Successful entrepreneurs run the full spectrum; from subteens to the very elderly. The entrepreneurial process does not limit those in any age group if they are motivated and get into motion.

Bob Dean made his first dollar when he was 12 years old. He sold candy for fund raisers. He started out making it at home and sold it at wholesale to his classmates. In six months he grossed $30,000! At 15, Dean bought a used Cadillac limo. He parlayed that into a limo firm that delivers Chief Executive Officers, three or four times his age, to business and social functions in both Washington, D.C. and Los Angeles. A few years ago, his company passed annual revenues of $2.6 million!

Just out of his teens and still in college, Mike Zeid started a leather shop. A few years later, Leather Loft stores were grossing $18 million a year!

When she was 21 years of age, Sophie Collier began selling her own homemade natural sodas from a pushcart. A few years later, her soda pop company had revenues in excess of $20 million!

Bill Gates quit Harvard without graduating. In his early twenties, Bill started a software company called Microsoft. Later Microsoft went to the public trough with a stock offering. It has been estimated on Wall Street that his stock is worth more than $1 billion!

When Jennifer Cherney was only 27 years of age, she closed over $150 million in real estate deals in New York City; that was several years ago!

Debbie Fields began her cookie corporation in her mid-twenties. She brought up her original idea of chewy chocolate-chip cookies and she was warned that it was a going-nowhere idea. Research had proven beyond any doubt that Americans like crispy cookies, not soft and chewy chocolate cookies. What did Debbie know? She ignored the advice and plunged ahead. Fields attributes her success to her father's advice,

"Be the best you can. Whatever you do, do it because you love it, *not because of money.*"

Fred Gibbons, founder of Software Publishing Corporation, became a
multimillionaire as he passed from his twenties to his thirties! Conrad
Hilton was 59 years old when he entered the hotel business! At age 64, Bob
Howell launched a "Private Mailbox Service." In a few years, he had 24
franchises sprinkled through the Seattle area! The late Colonel Sanders
was in his late sixties when he started Kentucky Fried Chicken! J.R.
Simplot, the venerable McDonald Frozen Idaho French Fried Potato entrepreneur, is in his eighties, active, and not counting the years! Grandma
Moses began to paint and sell when she was 90!

Venerable Casey Stengel once noted,

"They say you can't do it, But, sometimes, that
doesn't work."

Our country bubbles with teenage, in-the-twenties, and gray panther
entrepreneurs.

There are no limiting age factors.

Family

They hail from the rich parts of the city to poor ghettos. They come from
both sides of the track, broken homes, foster homes, country club estates,
and rock-stable families. Many were juvenile delinquents, Eagle scouts,
are recovering addicts, church goers, free spirits, and flower children.
Some come from illiterate parents; others from a long line of prestigious
Ph.D.'s.

George Dale Murray was abandoned by his parents when he was 3 years
old. He was set adrift with a poor stranger who barely had enough money
to feed him.

George owns the Chris-Craft boat company. He has 15 cars (7 of them
Mercedes), 3 jets, and employs 9 full-time pilots!

Worth more than $100 million, Murray acknowledges he has always
wanted to go to college, but he cannot spare the time!

With the beauty of a movie star and the brains of a business genius,

Nabila Khashoggi comes from a fabulously wealthy and intelligent family.

Nabila was president of her family's Triad Corporation and chairperson of other companies.

At the ripe age of 23, she had a personal fortune estimated as high as $1.5 billion.

Not long ago, she launched a new venture, Infolex, a computerized tourist information service.

Entrepreneurs come from all family backgrounds.

Environment

Startups have begun in a wide variety of environments and circumstances.

Lynette Vives emerged from a tough Brooklyn ghetto environment *sans* college degree. She was thirty and a stewardess when her airline suddenly furloughed her. Lynette started peddling software. In four years she owned a multimillion dollar software sales firm in the nation's capitol.

She says,

> "It's an all-American dream. But I didn't allow anything to stand in my way. There's nothing you can't have if you want it badly enough."

All environments spawn entrepreneurs.

Education

Education must be viewed as a valuable tool. It is equally important to know that it is no guarantee of success.

A recent entrepreneurial study indicated that the greatest number of successful entrepreneurs (about 40%) have graduated from college.

Kenneth Good struggled for three backbreaking years to put himself through college, working nights as a door-to-door salesman. A sympathetic professor helped him get his diploma through a scholarship. Twenty years later, self-made multimillionaire Kenneth Good set up a foundation to give away more than $25 million in scholarships over the next 10 years. He says that a college degree was the key to his success.

Louis Elwell III graduated from the prestigious Wharton School of Business with a Major in Finance and Entrepreneurial Studies. His grades were excellent! His credentials were imposing. Louis was inordinately successful and became president of a multimillion dollar energy conservation company in the international marketplace.

A general education and financial background are very desirable, but there are always glaring exceptions to such entrepreneurial paradigms.

At the other end of the spectrum was Charlie Schulz. He failed every single subject in the eighth grade!

Charlie flopped miserably and flunked most of his high school courses. He received a fat zero in Physics. It was widely known that Charlie Schulz was the school's worst physics student!

It was obvious he would bomb everything he tried, except maybe, drawing. With an unenviable educational record and unknown drawing skill, Schulz applied for work with the Walt Disney Studios. Of course he was turned down flat. But he stayed with his love for drawing. He became a drawing entrepreneur and persevered. He created a comic strip about a little boy whose kite would never fly. He called it "Peanuts." Charles Schulz marketed "Peanuts" and is now a multimillionaire entrepreneur! But you would never know Charlie could do it from reading his school report card grades or his educational credentials.

About 25% of all successful entrepreneurs have Master's degrees. Almost as many, 20%, have high school diplomas. Ph.D.'s are about 10% double the high school dropout rate of 5%. The 10% Ph.D. representation may not be a meaningful number because most Ph.D.'s train for research and teaching, not business venturing.

Note the following curve in Figure 2-1.

Clearly, no statement can be made about education with certainty. The overwhelming evidence shows that a college education is valuable and desirable, but no one should be deluded into thinking a college degree is an Annie Oakley to the winner's circle.

Lee Iacocca hit the nail on the head:

> "People say to me, 'You're a roaring success. How did you do it?' I go back to what my parents taught me. Apply yourself. *Get all the education you can.* But then, by God, do something! Don't just stand there! Make something happen!"

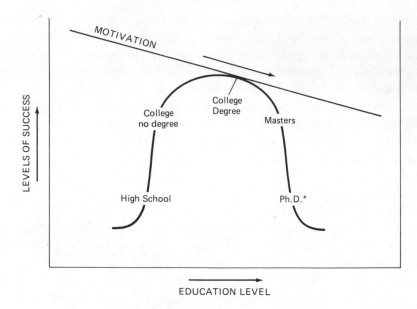

* It should be noted that most Ph.D.* candidates pursue their degree to teach or do research. Therefore, this is of little information.

Figure 2–1. Estimated education levels of successful entrepreneurs.

Dr. Joseph Mancuso of the Center of Entrepreneurial Management, discovered a little known, salient fact. The track record of entrepreneurial women differs from men. Though the average ages are in parallel, a higher percentage of successful female entrepreneurs hold Bachelor's degrees! In summation, schooling IS valuable. The bottom line is that it is a tool, nothing more. Get it and use it wisely, but YOU must make something happen!

Lifestyle

Entrepreneurs are aware of their minds and bodies.

They are mobile and proactive. Many are enthusiastic joggers, downhill skiers, tennis players, racquet ball enthusiasts, and cross country cyclists. Most get caught up and become committed to whatever they do.

Also, entrepreneurs migrate to startup groups and get caught up with creative and innovative people. This appears to be a paradox, for the road to entrepreneurial success can be such a lonely one. Starting a new venture does not lend itself easily to a family setting, for the lifestyle of entrepreneurs is hectic and demanding. Often family priorities fade into the background due to a total commitment to the startup. It requires a very understanding and cooperative spouse to tolerate a driven entrepreneur.

Do not tell that to entrepreneur Ken Ellred, an MBA from Stanford, who founded INMAC, a computer catalog company. Ken's experience in the catalog publishing business was *nil* prior to INMAC. Ellred was devoted to his family and to church. His love and devotion to his wife and children became a unique strength which impelled him to success. His dream quotient was high. His confidence was unflappable. He was Charlie Chaplinesque in his convictions.

INMAC went public and made Ken a multimillionaire before age 40. He still runs INMAC, and his family continues to lead the pack.

Entrepreneurs have an active lifestyle.

Personality

A fly in the entrepreneur make-up often appears to be compulsive behavior. The staccato demand to be right and the instant reaction frequently lead to making off-the-wall decisions, quitting a job impulsively instead of waiting it out, and general impetuosity. It is partly a reflection of their gear-up enthusiastic nature, intense desire to succeed, and rapid decision making under fire. Frequently, entrepreneurs have an unassailable optimism and confidence with answers to burn: that is a common fault. They must learn control and not shoot from the lip.

Moreover, most entrepreneurs have tunnel vision. It comes with the territory. They are not easily dissuaded.

Entrepreneurs tend to be extroverts. They must be careful of a fatal flaw which is to easily become infatuated with gimcracks, creative tricky products, complex machines, innovative methods, and unusual marketing gimmickry.

Because nearly 80% of all startups are product driven, some entrepreneurs become more focused on the product than the market.

The CEO of Inacomp Computer Centers once observed impishly,

> "The entrepreneur is a guy who is personally guaranteeing $5 million and has about $5 in his pocket."

Entrepreneurs have a wide variance in personality.

Persistence

If there is one behavioral glitch an entrepreneur must possess, develop, and practice it is persistence.

Successful entrepreneurs are dogged in their persistence. They never, never, never give up.

Ray Kroc carved out a world empire built on the McDonald hamburger.

In the beginning, he stumbled, picked himself up and moved forward. He met disappointment after disappointment and fought back against strong and determined competition.

Kroc persevered even when it appeared to others that all was lost.

Ray Kroc described persistence as his most valuable trait and the one most important for success. Entrepreneurs persist and persist and persist and persist.

Goals

Setting and reaching goals today, is the most appealing of all illusions. We read quick-fix books, trying to learn everything from real estate investing to weight loss in 10 days. There is a compelling sense of urgency only about the short term—the quick buck. We want a result, *pronto*. That is the sticky problem associated with new ventures. They are cash intensive and they become cash alligators. Moreover, investors want to know when the company is going to turn the corner, be profitable, and start a payback. Our present entrepreneur groupies are caught up in a hypergoal setting mode, a condition that frequently puts pressure on only the present and near horizon. The daily, weekly, and monthly progress reports are a dangerous quagmire associated with the startup. The long range perspective is held in low esteem. Near time startup problems are very challenging and demand immediate attention. The chaotic journey is not over until the calm, deep headwaters of maturity are reached. Many startup managers have such a mindset on the short term that they achieve quick profitability, ignoring the long range, build a weak customer base or a suboptimal product, and later, fall into despairing bankruptcy. To set goals is a necessity, and entrepreneurs must know or quickly learn the difference between the long and the short of it, as well as the imperatives of each.

What Yogi Bera mumbled, must be remembered,

"The game ain't over until it's over."

It is necessary to establish goals, but it is critical to wade through patiently to the end of the rainbow, which is in the far distance. Goals, of the long kind, are most important.

Experience

A research project by the University of Barcelona's Professor Juan Roure found discernible experience differences between successful and unsuccessful firms.

The founders of successful ventures had more prior experience working in the same industry as well as experience working together. With experience in hand—that elusive big-E—the entrepreneur has one leg up and can deal more effectively with uncertainty and the highly cluttered future.

Experience has always been an important building block in the intuition base for making sound judgments.

Noted Silicon Valley marketing champion, Regis McKenna, pegs intuition as,

> "Judgment based on experience."

Though entrepreneurs feel more secure with making judgment calls based on experience, in fact, that is still not the answer, for not all of the uncertainty has been eliminated. Some successful startups have been made without the benefit of experience. In the early 1970s, Jim Treybig, without experience, had an idea for a fault-free computer mainframe which would take on IBM. He recalled,

> "For three solid years, everybody told me I was
> crazy."

Jim felt he needed financial experience to make judgments about launching a fault-free computer mainframe. He found a job in the venture capital (V.C.) field. The V.C. Experience gave Treybig the background necessary.

TV talk show hostess Barbara Walters said,

> "Trust your gut."

That is what Treybig did. He leaned on his intuition and gut feel to birth the legendary, fault-free Tandem Computer company.

Kenneth Oshman and the founders at ROLM decided to enter the PBX field. They had experience working together but had zero experience in the telephone business. There was formidable competition possessing enormous resources. Oshman and his team pushed ahead anyway. The ROLM management parlayed the PBX new venture into a barn-burning success! A few years later, the company was sold to IBM for about $250 million!

The stories of no-experience new ventures are numerous and should be ignored.

Dean Watkins and Dick Johnson had no business experience or experience working together. Yet they founded a high technology company, Watkins-Johnson. Watkins-Johnson grew to be a highly regarded and successful international surveillance company in the Silicon Valley.

However, this is a rare occurrence and the chances of a repeat performance are remote. On the balance, experience, both in the field and working together, is regarded as a substantial headstart. It is the 80/20 rule once again with experience an 80% plus factor, but 20% will make it without either.

Some Success Stories

Entrepreneurs Are Motivated

Tom Monaghan, the Michigan pizza tycoon, owns Domino's Pizza and the Detroit Tigers baseball champions.

When he was five years old, Tom's father died. His mother shunted him to a Catholic orphanage. Tom graduated 44th in a high school class of 44 students! As Tom recalls,

> "I wasn't even supposed to graduate. But I went to the nun's house, copped a plea, and did a lot of crying. They passed me."

He had two "fathers" to raise him: Sister Bernarda, a nun at the orphanage, and Father Apasemo, after he left the orphanage.

> "They showed me I could bring good ethics and fair play into my business."

He owns Domino's Pizza privately. Its annual gross sales are well over $500 million, with more than 2000 stores worldwide. Tom Monaghan did not have the education, experience, or credentials. All he had was motivation, persistence, and ethics. By the way, Tom wants to let go of the reins at Domino's to devote more time and effort to his church.

Think Big

Willard Millard once drove trucks, dug ditches, dropped out of college, and founded two businesses which failed. Then he created ComputerLand, a worldwide chain of incredibly successful computer stores. A few years ago, according to Forbes Magazine, he was listed as having at least $600 million; one of the 400 richest persons in America! Millard said,

> "What is needed and wanted in the world, are people who will do what they say they'll do. *Keep your word. Think big, really think big!* If you have the courage to stand up and say that this is what I want to do, and do it, you can be successful.
> I see no one being successful doing something they didn't want to do."

Abruptly, he moved to Saipan in the Trust Territories in the Pacific, for tax reasons.

Henry David Thoreau wrote,

> "In the long run men hit only what they aim at. Therefore, because they could fail immediately, they had better aim high at something high."

You can be as BIG as you think.

Carve Out Niches

In 1980, Fred Gibbons was 29, Janelle Bedke 30, and John Page 35. All three left Hewlett Packard to start Software Publishing. Fred Gibbons ponied up his life savings, $50,000.

They worked out of their homes, no salary. That was sweat equity for the other two. Bedke wrote the user's manual. Page designed the first program. Gibbons hustled to get the products to market, the company off and running. The market niche was well identified. It was a segment unserved. The three plugged away relentlessly. The software publishing new venture was profitable within 12 months! Janelle will tell you,

> "This is not a hit business. You don't depend on some creative genius to come up with your next 1-2-3. And it isn't magic."

Janelle has a formula for success:

> "If you set good marketing and operations plans and execute them, you can be a successful, profitable long-term software company. You must have a good, focused but broad-based, strategy."

Software Publishing went public in 1984 with a stock valuation of over $40 million.

Run Lean And Mean

Aryeh Finegold was a totally committed company commander during the fighting in Israel's 1967 and 1973 wars. According to Aryeh,

> "All my boys came back. I didn't lose a man. A lot of it was luck. Same in business. Only .01% is doing the right thing and things right. All it takes is goofing off that little bit and it's enough to kill you. In business, nobody takes prisoners."

He was also founder of Daisy Systems Corporation in Mountain View, California. His commitment was again, total. Not long after the IPO, the company had $85 million in working capital, sitting in the bank. The biggest problem Finegold faced was managing rapid growth. There had been three successful public offerings (IPOs). With money stowed in the coffers, Finegold decided to take on another startup challenge. Finegold's golden rules are:

"First, pick an ever expanding market. Second, be
first to market. Third, be a leader."

Make It Against Odds

Still in his early twenties, John H. Breck combed through medical journals
looking for a cure for his hair loss.

He recognized an opportunity waiting to be grabbed. John Breck developed lotions and other products for the scalp. Proudly, he proclaimed he
could restore hair. John then opened his first scalp treatment center. Breck
expanded rapidly, losing his own hair on the way!

When he died in 1963, multimillionaire John Breck was America's
number one hair care and shampoo maker.

He was also bald!

Swing With Randomness

Not too long ago, Dee Brown wanted to start a business he could run just
part time. Dee wanted to spend time with his loves—music and painting.
He founded the Drapery Factory. Brown chose price sensitive buyers of
quality draperies as his target market segment. He rounded up a team of
decorators, all working out of their homes. It reduced costs which Dee
passed on to customers.

The Drapery Factory's prices were 5–15% below department stores
because of Dee's lower overhead. Quality was excellent.

His company took off and grew rapidly. Drapery Factory, Inc. was soon
making more than $2 million a year.

Brown came face to face with the horns of a dilemma. He had created
a drapery monster which had to grow rapidly or fade into obscurity. There
was no halfway. With the time demands of rapid growth would go his
beloved music and painting. Dee had to make an agonizing choice. Draperies tipped the scale. He expanded into the fast growth mode. The Drapery
Factory's gross revenues doubled and profits soared. How did it all come
about? According to Dee Brown, it was luck, a random happening.

Do Not Plan On Luck And Timing

The two-factor theory of luck and timing pervades every new venture. The
theory holds that both timing and luck are each impossible to anticipate

and not well understood. Hinda Schreiber-Miller and Lisa Zobian-Lindahl were two marathon runners. A product idea developed from the needs of the two joggers, both amply endowed. They searched for breast support in a jogging bra and could not find one on the market. "I wanted it," Zobian-Lindahl reasoned, "so everybody else must." The two of them designed a joggers' bra. Schreiber-Miller borrowed $5000 from her family. She found a South Carolina manufacturer to make 40 dozen bras. From the beginning, the business leaped to a fast start. They were right on track: the timing was excellent. In the first year, JBI, Inc. earned $30,000.

Growing at 20% a year, annual sales increased to $3 million. Funding was needed for expansion and growth demands. They borrowed $25,000 more from the family. The Small Business Administration kicked in $50,000. Luck was fortuitous and the timing exquisite. The joggers line grew to take on sports briefs for women and support underwear for men, among other items.

Schreiber-Miller said,

> "We were lucky because, at least, we knew we didn't know business."

They often called on the University of Vermont School of Business for advice in solving business problems.

Entrepreneurs Are Promoters

Mike Sands was in his early thirties, and he wanted to start a cheesecake company. Mike decided to go for it! He launched, *C'est Cheesecake.*

He was down to eight bucks in his pocket. It was enough to cover the cost of ingredients for one special cheesecake. Sands displayed an uncanny knack for media-grabbing. That made the difference. On National Chocolate Chip Cookie Day, he gave away bags of white chocolate chip cookies, appeared on five Los Angeles radio stations, all to promote his cheesecake. In a few years, with promotion savvy, a quality product, and a well understood market, the business grossed over $5 million. Another key to Sands' success in promoting his cheesecake was complete confidence in his product. Mike Sands continued to be the consumate promoter. He places enormous faith in free promotion gimmicks of every and any kind.

Go Against The Trend

John Scheck was a skilled weekend woodworker. With four colleagues he formed Giga-tronics in 1980. They spent the first three months scrubbing, sheetrocking, and hand building desks, work benches, and office partitions. They even carved the outdoor sign! The development of a unique, digitally controlled microwave signal generation and measurement instrument was their product strategy. Giga-tronics' initial staff of 7 spent 18 months developing the prototype for alpha testing. An R&D venture capital partnership provided $350,000. Later, an additional $610,000 was pumped in. They continued R&D until they had the product right. Then Giga-tronics hit it. They were designated as a sole R&D supplier to the U.S. Navy for digitally controlled microwave signal generators.

Five years later, sales scooted past $40 million and Giga-tronics earned almost $8 million. Consider a not-long-ago financial recap. Half of Giga-tronics' equity was in current assets. The other half was in cash or liquid short-term investments.

Giga-tronics proved to be one of California's most spectacular high tech new ventures. They had defied the conventional strategy by being product driven, not market driven. Scheck said,

> "There's no question, our product strategy was superb."

At the last check, the handmade desks, sheetrock, carpentry, and sign were still in place.

Entrepreneurs Are Rebels With A Passion

George Malekos had always been a Rebel With a Passion: a hellbent, pigheaded loner who made tracks. Malekos set out for the Alaska frontier in search of freedom, independence, and to make his fortune. Eagle River was just a layover point in the wilderness when he arrived. He was standing in the middle of town when a bolt-of-lightning idea hit him. George knew how he could make his fortune! Build a restaurant right in the center of this town! It cannot miss! What a location! location! location! With a grubstake of $3000, Malekos bootstrapped it. He began broiling hamburgers out of a small, rented (shake of the hand) trailer. Before long he was in his own restaurant. George's North Slope & Sophie's Oyster Bar was soon a packed eatery. It was not long before he employed 114 work-ers, seated 1,500 patrons a day in three different dining rooms, and boasted the biggest chandelier this side of Anchorage! Stop there? No. A hotel or a parking garage looked like another placer load opportunity. The truth of George Malekos is that he has an eagle eye for finding golden veins. A Rebel With a Passion, he rapidly fills an opportunity lode, after checking for Kodiak bear in hibernation.

SOME COMMON MYTHS

Entrepreneurs Are Born, Not Made

Biographies of successful entrepreneurs often read as if they entered the world with an extraordinary genetic endowment. Then they worked at mini-startups from age six until they were multimillionaires. It is a pat story. But there are almost as many counter tales of those who made the hit on the entrepreneur jackpot without the benefit of genetics. Their traits and genetics do not fall into any sensible pattern for startup successes. Dr. Modesto Maidique lists the genetic factor as important but not exclusive. There is a serendipity of unpredictable events that does not have much to do with family heritage. Successful new ventures are as much the result of a driving entrepreneur with an abundance of luck and timing.

On the balance, it is desirable to come from two learned, successful entrepreneurial parents. It is also beneficial to gain work experience and get adequate education. That scenario will substantially enhance the prob-ability of success.

So many factors are unrelated to genetics and support the countering paradigm that:

Entrepreneurs are often made, not born!

Entrepreneurs Are Not Fired

A recent study of entrepreneurs has shown that about 80% have been fired at one time or another. Entrepreneurs are nonconformists and find it difficult to be "team players." Some are misfits, not suited for the job in which they are placed. Others are so individualistic as to not conform. An observation is accurate that entrepreneurs are restless, not stuck hard and fast in any job other than a startup. Product manufacturing companies have an inordinate rate of personnel migration due to a high pressure cooker environment, unrelated to entrepreneurs. They are often fired from firms because of their roving-mind mentality. It is not a reflection of their abilities.

Consider Albert Fuller, fired from his first three jobs!

He was a streetcar conductor in Boston. Fuller was fired for taking unauthorized control of a car, wrecking it. As a stable hand, he was fired a second time for being careless with his master's horse. As a messenger, Albert was fired for a third time for losing too many packages. Then he started selling brushes door to door. When his boss ignored housewives' complaints, he went into business for himself.

The Fuller Brush man story and mountain climb is legendary. Fuller persisted to scale Everest-like heights of success. Getting fired was probably the best thing that ever happened to Albert Fuller.

Entrepreneurs Are Job Hoppers

A good argument can be made that entrepreneurs are highly mobile and volatile. But workers in startups who job hop are not necessarily entrepreneurs. In Silicon Valley it has been recorded that there is a turnover of one third of the workforce each year. Workers will transfer to another company, be fired, or just leave. Some entrepreneurs take an unwanted departure due to internal friction as Steven Jobs did at Apple. There are many other founders who have brought in professional management, fell into immediate conflict, and departed. Most entrepreneurs are in motion. If they are highly motivated, however, it has been found they can stay with a job for several years.

That is proven when they start their own business. Successful entrepreneurs display the ability to hang in there for the long and torturous startup grind.

R. David Thomas was a high school dropout. He lacked stick-to-it-ness. With good reason, his adoptive father warned Thomas that he would never make it because he could not stick it out with a job for long. R. Dave began as a delivery boy. Then he founded Wendy's Restaurants. His hamburger empire reached 3500 plus restaurants in over 20 countries. A few years ago, Wendy's earned more than $76 million. He is still there.

Entrepreneurs Do Not Have Bad Ideas

That is what Norman Mailer calls a factoid, an "imagined fact."

In a first promotional scheme, Karl Benz drove his newly patented Motorwagen 200 miles to a trade show in Munich. The only buyer interested enough to order one of Benz's 3-wheeled, 1-cylinder automobiles was committed to an insane asylum before he could take delivery. That sale was a bad idea!

Edsel, foam-filled tires, quadrophonic stereos, infrared night vision devices for autos, Speedwalks, Jolt Cola, the Peanut by IBM, and a mechanized Toy Rat were among hundreds of bad ideas.

Adam Osborne designed the first portable computer. The Osborne computer pancaked into bankruptcy. His next new venture was Paperback Software, presently growing at a reasonable rate. It is Adam's contention that entrepreneurs must experience a dozen bad ideas before a good one makes any economic sense.

An entrepreneur, Rob Reis, wrote,

> "Do not let your failure stop you! You can come
> back if you try again and again and again and again."

Scott McNealy, one of the founders of Sun Microsystems, is said to have a new idea each day. Many were bad ideas as he will tell you, but enough have been good ideas to make him a multi-millionaire.

Most important, entrepreneurs have ideas!

Entrepreneurs Are Charismatic

A study of hundreds of successful entrepreneurs suggests that few correspond to having "divine inspiration," as "aura bound," have "charisma," or possess that "grace under stress" we associate with JFK and Churchill.

Entrepreneurs are simply people-people; sometimes go-go persons, humdrum characters, occasionally nervous, ofttimes calm, occasionally fuss-budgets or detail averse, confident or insecure, and electrifying or dull.

Some entrepreneurs blend and fade in crowds. Nothing sets them apart from average pedestrians on the sidewalk. They often appear as amiable flukes or country bumpkins.

Entrepreneurs Are Inflexible

If entrepreneurs are anything, they are too loose and notoriously flexible. They must be, for they function in an environment of radical, constant change. They have to develop nifty footwork and learn to feint, dodge constantly, and roll with new venture punches. Entrepreneurs are mental jugglers. There is rarely, no, never, only one answer in the entrepreneurship process. Entrepreneurs are whacked on the sides of the head with opposing ideas and kicked in the seat of the pants with a third.

In all cases, they must be flexible, according to Stanford's Professor Bob Keeley, or end up waistdeep in deep night soil.

Peters and Waterman both put emphasis on flexibility,

> "The ultimate entrepreneurial strategic weapon is flexibility."

Entrepreneurs Are Logical

Entrepreneur imaginations run rampant. They believe they can scale the highest obstacle. Because their horizon has no limit, they are often logically illogical. The key to the success of many entrepreneurs may be their kooky ability to think "illogically," consider the most capricious of ideas, then make them into "logical" outcomes. Many "illogical" ideas have evolved into successful startups; Pong, Frisbie, Hoola Hoop, Pet Rock, Cabbage Patch Dolls, Madonna, Residence Inns, as examples.

Entrepreneurs Follow The Rules

They are rule-resistors. They bend, twist, and break rules. Entrepreneurs are, by nature, renegades and dissenters. They abhor the norm. They reject toeing any line but their own. Most are disruptive. It is fact that many revolutionary ideas are disconcerting, upset the accepted order and tradition, and break the fixed patterns to become innovative and successful startup ideas. When they get started, many times they cannot put the brakes on, and zoom right through the STOP signs.

Bill Foster, founder of Stratus Computers, has a paradigm:

> "Rules are for rulers. Whatever works is for entrepreneurs."

Entrepreneurs Set Sights Too High

Professor Michael Ray of Stanford suggests,

> "If your idea gets laughed at, you might be on to something."

Entrepreneurs keep shooting for the high stuff and the stars. That is why it has always been and should be! One of the most successful new ventures is Ben & Jerry's Ice Cream, started by Jerry Greenfield and Ben Cohen. Jerry said,

> "The best advice I received was from Ben Cohen. When somebody tells you that something can't be done, all it really means is that it hasn't been done before!"

Entrepreneurs, who are the most successful, are those who are constantly reaching, sending a high C to the peanut gallery in the third balcony. Rarely do entrepreneurs aim low. That is why wary investors apply a "fudge factor" of three or four, plus or minus, to every forecast an entrepreneur makes.

Consider Bob Haft, founder of Crown Brooks, who contends there are no limits in entrepreneuring. He says,

> "Listen, *dream,* study, experiment, tinker, and excell."

Dorothy sang the entrepreneur's song,

> "Somewhere, over the rainbow, bluebirds fly. Birds fly over the rainbow. Why, oh why, can't I?"

Silicon Valley harbors many successful entrepreneurs who had their eye focused on a target out of sight to others and made it all the way.

Entrepreneurs Are Hard Workers

Hard work should not be confused with smart work. It is possible to carry the hard work ethic to excess.

During one of his lucid moments, Howard Hughes said,

"I work smart, not hard."

Hard hours are often confused as necessary for achievement. There is a great deal of daylight between them. Most successful entrepreneurs learn to work smart instead of hard and accomplish more.

At a Cañada College entrepreneur seminar in California, six successful entrepreneurs, from 26 to 55 years of age, admitted they were diligent golfers, tennis buffs, daily joggers, or committed racketball players. All acknowledged they were smart workers, not hard workers.

Every one of the six selfmade entrepreneurs said time for their family was a number one priority, recreation as number two, and work as number three. One was a Ph.D., three graduated from college, and two made it through high school. Mervin Morris did not make it to college. He founded Mervyn's Department Stores. He was also a daily jogger. By the way, a marketing expert convinced him that "Mervyn's" was better than "Mervin's." In the beginning, he worked long and hard, and worked smart.

Later, he learned how to work smart hours only. Anytime one of Mervin's children phoned, the call was immediately put through directly to Mervin, no matter where he was. He had his priority ducks in a row. Mervin was the epitome of the smart worker ethic. Morris was reputed to have received $300 million when he sold out. Energetic entrepreneur Mervin could not sit still for long, cutting coupons. He soon became involved in another profitable new venture, Ross Department Stores.

Many entrepreneurs take short refreshing "sabbaticals." Smart ideas are born during odd times, when smelling the roses, relaxing by the pool in a Barwa chair, watching paint dry, or rolling on the grass. Remember, the Pareto Rule of 80/20 supports the tenet that executives spend 20% of their time on 80% of the problems. That is smart working.

Irv Tague proved that. He took over a battered, almost bankrupt regional airline, Airwest, for Howard Hughes. It was so deep in hock, Tague had enough money for only 11 days operation with the tacit understanding there was no help forthcoming from Howard. He started from scratch. His team labored heroically. Tague spun Hughes Airwest (HAW) around in a year. Irv usually came into the office five days a week, at around 10 A.M., and left about 2 P.M. He spent the balance of the time around his pool in Portola Valley, a portable phone in his hand. Every year Tague and his smart Big-4 management team ran Hughes Airwest, profits were in the millions. Midway Airlines was his second new venture. It was a hub-and-spoke airline concept out of little-used Midway airport on Chicago's South side. It grew into a cash cow, the most successful startup in airline history!

The message of Irving Tague is,

> "Use whatever system that works."

Connectair was to be Tague's third skyrocketting venture—a connecting regional carrier based at Ontario Airport on the West Coast. It blew both engines and coughed to a calamitous stop.

Flex-time is an acknowledgment that greater output can ease the crunch and more accomplished with flexible smart hours than hard clock hours.

SOME UNCOMMON TRUTHS

Entrepreneurs Learn From Other Innovators

An old Chinese adage might be rephrased.

> "A good entrepreneur goes straight—round in a circle."

Networking and interacting with people who have been involved in innovation, digging into the cheap experience basket, and building a resource coalition, is a worthwhile endeavor. That is Tom Peters straight talk. Researcher Brian Quinn came up with research which supports Nancy Austin writing in "Passion For Excellence":

> "A major new product has never come from a formal planning process."

James Utterback found that about half of all information that stimulated innovations came from someone other than the innovator! One can get a tremendous amount of insightful information from those who have done it, just for the asking. Innovators who have been over the course are usually free with their advice and like to chat about it. Information and strategic alliances come from random sources and under the most casual circumstances. Sometimes chitchat at the club, at a bar, next to the watercooler, on the commuter train, or at a PTA meeting will provide a contact that grows into a sterling new venture.

Entrepreneurs Are Motivated

Successful entrepreneurs do not depend on others to do the job. They know that they can do it! They are motivated to carry the responsibility all of the way to Newcastle.

Ultra-famous chocolatier Milton Hershey knew more about candy-making and motivation than he did about business. The motivated entrepreneur had to overcome several failed ventures before introducing Milk Chocolate Bars and Kisses that would make a fortune and become signature products.

Von Braun developed a rocket in 1942. He made 65,121 changes in the "final" model. It failed 23 of the 29 tests. He determined another 5,000 changes had to be made.

Because of his motivation, Von Braun succeeded.

Successful entrepreneurs have confidence in their abilities, make a solid commitment, and say it time and again, every day.

Entrepreneurs Are Visionaries

They have visions, not always crystal clear. They see the big picture far into the future. A clear vision in the distance to entrepreneurs is often only a blur to others.

When he was young, Conrad Hilton's mother said to him,

"If you want to launch big ships, you have to go where the water is deep."

"They don't bunt" is the observation of entrepreneur and advertising wizard, David Ogilvy. Entrepreneurs have focused visions of grandeur. They have their goals in crosshair sight, and a unique ability to keep a sharp eye on their target, and do not waver.

Entrepreneurs Are Strategy Oriented

"Guesstimating" the future is no easy task. Entrepreneurship is easier with a defined strategy. The fact that it is a roll of the dice, and entrepreneurs have to cope. Conditions under which a strategy is developed, change irrationally the following day, and this cannot be anticipated. Radical change is an integral part and parcel of a strategy. Remember, it was not raining when Noah built the Ark, but he had a strategy.

That brilliant futuristic thinker, Herman Kahn said,

> "All we know about the future is that it will be different from the present."

That is why an entrepreneur must have a strategy and a course of action, in any case.

The founder of the highly successful Popeye's Famous Fried Chicken and Biscuits is entrepreneur Al Copeland. His advice is,

> "Plan for what happens when you succeed and plan for what happens when you fail. Planning is the most important thing."

Here is another paradigm worth living by,

> "The absence of a plan is unacceptable."

Entrepreneurs Spot Opportunities

There are opportunities abounding all over the countryside. For example, business consultants say, in every problem there is an opportunity. It takes an entrepreneurial eye to see the opportunity, seize, and exploit it. Again, about J. R. Simplot, the frozen french-fried potato king of McDonald's Hamburger fame. He invested $20 million and established Micron Technology to challenge the Japanese in their clear-advantage speciality of mass producing memory chips. He did not know he could not win, for he was a visionary. In time, Micron recorded earnings of $4 million a month. Simplot baffled the experts by winning.

He said,

> "If you wait till all the information is in, the opportunity is always past. Wait long enough and you can become an expert."

He knew an "expert" rarely starts a new venture. It is more often an "inexpert," which he was.

The message is straightforward: do not linger. Time is aflying and wonderful opportunities scoot, dart, weave, and flit by. Just do not wait until it seems that everything will work out in a straight line for it will not.

In Megatrands, John Naisbitt wrote,

> "Gee-whiz futurists are always wrong because they believe that technological innovation travels in a straight line. It doesn't. It weaves and bobs and sputters."

Entrepreneurs Find Superior Talents

The successful entrepreneur knows the people in the company will make or break it. Therefore, the highest qualified people are the most desirable strategy. Successful entrepreneurs get top-gun talent on board. That is one step closer to ensuring the success of a startup. Obtaining the finest talent is personified when the team members are more skilled in their discipline than the founder. The canny entrepreneur can then step back and leave the turf to them to get on with it. That is more David Ogilvy stuff!

It is what Sandra Kurtzig did at ASK Computer Systems. She chose an "ace" group of managers and moved aside to give her super management team,

> "Enough rope to see if they could do the job."

For a long time, ASK increased sales at a high double digit rate annualized.

On former President Reagan's desk was a plaque which said,

> "There's no limit to what you can do if you don't mind who gets the credit."

Entrepreneurs Are Doers

He who hesitates is lost? One of the biggest pitfalls to avoid in the business arena is "mañana," the little-bit-later ethic. Then it is followed up with in-the-nick-of-time management.

Good managers practice Management By Objectives (MBO).

The riskiest attitude is the waiting game, until all the information is in. Fred Smith, founder of one of the gangbuster startups in this century, Federal Express, is a champion of the MBO ethic. He says,

"Do one thing at a time, but do it, *and now!*"

The noted writer, Thomas Aldous Huxley wrote,

"The great end of life is not knowledge but action."

Entrepreneurs Are On The Job Trainees

Would-be entrepreneurs have fantasies about how to do a startup. They read avidly on the subject.

Studying how-to-do-it books is like reading The Joy Of Sex hoping to suddenly become a kinky sex symbol and an expert on applied sex. A how-to-do-it book makes a contribution. It can serve a large purpose, as does networking for information, familiarization, and direction. It is important to do for it provides a tool, a road map, a guide, and a recipe that is useful. Hands-on, do-it-yourself, and on-the-job training is the only way to learn the truth and get the job done. There are no shortcuts, no substitutes for doing, certainly not between book covers. Too much reading can turn the information into the value of a six pack. Ask major U.S. corporations which have had markets throw their market-studded product back at them, even after exhaustive, sophisticated research called "Analysis to paralysis." They discovered only by getting their feet wet. No matter how much planning, calculating, studying, networking, and prestart research takes place, worthwhile results come from the doing. Ford found about the Edsel by doing. NeXT discovered its flaws by doing. By getting the product to the market, the market will echo its support or distaste through the most valid of all feedback, sales. Successful entrepreneurs "manage by walking around—outside," as Peter Drucker has written. They set up marketing monitoring procedures and feedback tactics. They let the market guide them by the hand. It is demeaning work—difficult and the only way. It is also peon labor.

The lot of an entrepreneur is as Tom Edison aptly put it,

> "One percent inspiration and ninety-nine percent perspiration."

An entrepreneur must be willing to launch a project, be a gofer, encourage constructive dissension, nurture feedback, deal swiftly with the inconsistencies, experience elation, suffer deflation, ignore the fat ego, and press on. The brass ring for the entrepreneur to grab in a new venture is pure exhileration. It is up to the person!

Ted Turner said it loud and clear,

> "For me, life is an adventure—you know, like the yellow brick road. I want to see what Oz is like. Life IS an adventure. So why shouldn't we have a good time? This is America. You can do anything here!"

3
WHY BECOME AN ENTREPRENEUR?

A SEASON FOR ALL REASONS

The most compelling reason for becoming an entrepreneur is to accomplish something—for you! It is to build something from nothing, to make a dream come true!

It has been said,

> "If you have the strength to dream, you also have the
> strength to make the dream come true."

The realization of a dream and the chance to do something about it is one of the inalienable rights of the entrepreneur. Thomas Jefferson said it another way,

> "Freedom is the right to choose."

The freedom to choose a startup is not an easy one. There are many roadblocks: personal, financial, and emotional. The end rewards of entrepreneurship are uncertain under the most favorable conditions. The entrepreneur has to come to grips with the reality that choosing a new venture is a madcap excursion, a fantasy voyage into the unknown, and many people may be dragged along. Rewards in accomplishment and money are very appealing. Accomplishment is satisfaction with a job well done, for most. Money typically plays a minor motivating role, though it is a major consideration and strong motivating force for some. The hard dollars involved at first are real, yet the future monetary rewards are ethereal and indefinite. That is why the dollar sign hangs below the sky-hook of accomplishment. The freedom to choose, as stated by Jefferson, is a knack for sensing opportunities where others see crises, danger, chaos, and confusion. The Chinese symbols for crisis and opportunity are identical. Literally translated, it reads,

> "Crisis is an opportunity riding on a dangerous wind."

To choose is the bundling together of a founding team to work harmoniously. It includes the skill to find, generate, and marshall resources: then make it all fall in place. The "why" of becoming an entrepreneur can be motored by other subsets of accomplishment and monetary considerations.

LUST FOR POWER

In a survey conducted with Harvard Business School students, 80% interviewed said that they were planning to start their own businesses for one major reason,

> They *lusted for power* to do it right!

They said,

> "Many of us believe that we would do things differently if we had the power. Most of us have a burning lust for power. We know that with power, we can grease the wheels to make things run smoother and more efficiently."

Oh, if only we had the power, we could do it so much better! That is the siren's wailing, an enticing song. Some persons work diligently for a firm.

Then they become frustrated with the infighting and the bickering. They find they are powerless to move the ten ton truck of resistance, doing it "the way we have for twenty years." There is a granite inertness, the defensive "don't rock the boat" policies, the corrosive inefficiencies, and the biting negatives. Persons working in that kind of environment are prime candidates for going out on their own where they can effect change.

Professor Karl Vesper, Chairman of the Management Department at the University of Washington in Seattle, said,

> "If necessity is the mother of invention, discontent is
> the mother of entrepreneurship."

As the discontented cup runneth over, closet entrepreneurs are compelled to break out on their own.

Consider J. Drapkin of Bladensburg, Maryland. He left a frustrating supervisory job to begin a telecommunications and marketing consulting firm. Drapkin said,

> "I left my job because I wanted the chance to do
> things the way I knew they should be done."

The lust for power and to be "master of the ship" syndrome was persuasive and strong. Drapkin's telecommunications and marketing consultancy firm evolved as a profitable and successful new venture.

Linda Hayes was bored with the triviality of her accounting job. She designed a computer program that would handle humdrum accounting tasks and do them right. She had trouble finding takers in her company. Linda realized the only way she could make things happen was to have her own company with the power to get things done efficiently. Not long ago, Hayes started a software company at the age of 25. Soon Linda had 80 employees on her company roster with more than 500 clients. Her software company chalked up over $10 million in annual sales.

There are also some who lust for power merely to gain respect of peers. Bill Regardie was terminated from six different jobs.

He began questioning his ability, as others seem to have done. Bill had to find out if he was all wrong. Openly, he lusted for the power to prove everyone else was wrong and he was right. He also wanted to change the world around him. Regardie decided the best way to do it was to publish a zingy real estate magazine. Why a real estate magazine? He explained it this way,

> "I had outgrown Playboy and Esquire Magazines. I
> didn't want to be a Washington weekly. No one was
> writing for me. No one was writing for the Fat Cat.
> I like to read about *Money, Greed, and Power!*"

He also lusted for the power that comes with being in the lead, Head Honcho, and King of the Hill! Starting with $5000, he went to work. The magazine took off like a rocket! It was not long after, Bill was offered $12 million for his sassy magazine with the name of Bill Regardie plastered on the cover extolling Money, Greed, and Power! He emerged as undisputed *enfant terrible* of the Washington publishing scene and wore his power as a boutonniere.

Over and over, it has been proven there is little wrong with lusting for power: wanting to be the boss. The problem is not getting power, it is what we do with it that is pivotal. Power can become an intoxicant. We must recognize that with power, the dune buggy ride begins. Power must be used smartly, for predators are everywhere. Sharpshooters taking pot shots are in blinds all over the landscape. They are ruthless, conniving, and shameless shooters.

The gift of power is fragile and can be lost in the wink of an eye. One must be prepared for jealousy, backbiting, chaos, agony, ecstasy, highs, lows, trauma, resistance, disappointment, elation, and a lot more. We can only keep reaching, higher and higher. There is no fall back, only a total collapse, and it is an awful dunk. The lust for power is not for the timid!

EGO AND THE ENTREPRENEUR

Egos in entrepreneurship are, by and large, not well understood. A writer noted in Forbes Magazine,

> "Show me an entrepreneur and I will show you an
> ego as long as Halley's Comet."

Werner Erhard's "So what?" comes to mind.

As entrepreneurs are highly mobile individuals, perhaps with an outward confidence and some inward insecurities. They are driven creatively, 12-speed goers, and with a sense of urgency. Their super-confidence may be verbalized *ad nauseum*, popping up everywhere, and that is not bad. Most entrepreneurs have egos to match the gleaming drive in their eyes, from gossamer visions of starting hundred buck small holes in back alleys to multimillion dollar multinational conglomerates. Egos and drive and entrepreneurs seem to fit like peas in a pod. This is part and parcel of a can-do generation.

John Jakes wrote in *North and South,*

"The race is to the driven, not the swift."

A solid state ballet danseuse, Kyra Nichols, said,

"This sounds really conceited, but whatever you ask
me to do, I can do."

That is not conceit, it is a well-supported ego of a driven person, not necessarily swift.

Steve Jobs was not aware of how big his goals and ego were when he became involved in Apple. His goals and ego were well within limits because of his ability to deliver. Steve did not flaunt his ego nor did he abuse it. He swam with the tide and Apple Computer proved to be one of the phenomenal startups of the century! Job's new NeXT computer venture is a luge run at an encore performance. His well-endowed ego is a plus, built upon his incredible success at Apple. He hopes NeXT will propel him to lofty heights the second time around. As the chips are falling in place, Jobs now has Perot, Cannon, and IBM as financial partners.

Nolan Bushnell is a classic example of a large ego and abounding confidence. Neither is worn ostentatiously nor objectionably. He is Perpetual Motion. No market, no challenge is too much for this free spirit. He exudes confidence in his springy walk.

Some wag observed that if a-new-idea-twice-a-day Bushnell ever came to a screeching halt, he would slide for two days! His ego provides a deep well of ideas. It is a robust motivator and positive force. When Nolan tried to sell one of his first video game concepts, he was told paddle games were out. Egocentric Busnell did not cowtow to the market wizards' alchemy.

He built a prototype anyway and named it, "Breakout." Everyone who played the video game became hooked on it. "Breakout" was a smash hit!

Gene Amdahl is one of the most flambouyant and confident entrepreneurs in the country. The Amdahl Company was an incredible new venture in the annals of startups. Venture capital funds poured in. Unfortunately, Amdahl's product and company did not flourish as anticipated. Under fire, Gene departed, only to start another company called Trilogy. Trilogy was recorded as one of the largest venture fundings in the history of venture capital; again, without a product, only a concept! It was estimated more than $250 million in venture funds backed Amdahl's Trilogy. That one did not get far out of the starting gate before it stumbled. Once again, the brilliant scientist is on his third startup, Andor. The jury is still out on Andor, but the wheels of progress are spinning. Amdahl has the right to wear an ego medallion on his lapel.

The three ventures are a tribute to his reputation, credentials, ego, and confidence. He can easily tap into the great venture capital funding pipeline in the sky. The cash register always rings for Gene Amdahl. Why? Because of this former head of IBM's Research & Development department's awesome credentials, quiet ego, and sublime confidence.

Xavier Roberts, 30, was a multimillionaire before Coleco marketed his Cabbage Patch Dolls. The Cabbage Patch Dolls were a shoo-in as far as Xavier was concerned. Roberts was dead certain the Dolls would scoop the market, and they did. Then he envisioned a recreation theme park of the Walt Disney genre. That was to be his next project. He claimed,

> "You have to shoot for the stars and keep shooting
> and shooting."

Egos just never die. They do not even fade away. They turn into new startups! A well-endowed ego is a tour de force that has boosted most entrepreneurs forward in the face of adversity. Entrepreneurship is a behavioral threatening undertaking. Continuing highs, compliments, and strokes tend to inflate an ego. A problem arises when an ego is malformed by the press and fellow adulators.

The id becomes destructive when the ego grows into an inflated ego, that stuff made of hot air. It fouls the entrepreneur's perception of the real world. When the ego is overblown, it ends up in loud, self-effacing, abrupt, abrasive, and blind-sided actions. The entrepreneur and ego are out of synch. The entrepreneur cannot deliver what the ego promised.

Sylvester Stallone had four box office smashes and then followed with two bombs. Did his ego get too inflated from the first four to twist his perception of what he was capable of doing? Did he believe his own PR? It is possible.

Keeping an ego in line requires constant monitoring with feet firmly planted on the turf. It is maintaining humility. It is a deaf ear to servile compliments: objectivity, reality. It means keeping one's head on straight when all around is spinning. Make no mistake, an ego is an impelling force when under control.

THRILL OF THE CHASE

It is the thrill of the chase, far more than the capture, that is exhilerating. Many entrepreneurs discover the new venture process is its own reward. The doing is a high; reason enough for becoming an entrepreneur. To pursue the fox over the hill and dale is the upper. Catching the fox is a downer.

Ben Sweetland wrote,

"Success is a journey, not a destination."

There are those with a single ambition, the pursuit of excellence, to effect change, and to create value; with no other goals in mind. They are the ones with a passionate desire to make something work, make a tangible contribution to society, and even make the world a better place to live. Some entrepreneurs are highly energized during the chase only to suffer ennui when the product reaches the market and the company begins to behave like a grown one. Entrepreneurs who can cope with a mature company are few and far between. They have to learn to deal with the rancor of the capture; the sluggishness of maturity, and the ensuing dearth of challenges. Remember the saga of ROLM which sold out when the chase was over and it began to behave like a mature company. For CEO Oshman, the challenge was gone. Ken stepped down with elegant dignity, his wallet bulging. Before long, Oshman put together a Leveraged Buyout Offer (LBO) package to buy Ampex and attempt a turnaround. Never mind that he had more than $50 million in his piggy bank. It was the challenge that moved Ken, not money.

The attempted acquisition did not pan out, so Oshman moved on to another challenge. He is now involved in Echelon, another high tech startup.

RUNNING IN PLACE

So often, the trivia patter around the water cooler is rife with expectations. The plan is pumped up to grand proportions without taking that first step. No risk there. At some time the water cooler chatter runneth dry. Everyone's thirst has been quenched. The spigot is turned off. It is the time to get off the dime. Listen to Isaac Walton and "Fish or cut bait." The Fat Lady has sung. You are on. Perform. The water is deepening. Sink or Swim. Drill the ball down the alley. Now! Get on the skateboard and skate! If we wait until the project is thoroughly investigated and evaluated, we can end up with analysis paralysis, wondering why the window of opportunity slammed shut. Dr. Tom Greening, a UCLA psychologist, admonishes,

> "Be a doer—not a stewer!"

The end thought is that it is better to have entrepreneured and lost, than not to have entrepreneured at all. Waiting in the wings is for daydreamers, not performers. Some have said that one is not a failure if the venture did not make it. An entrepreneur is a success for having tried.

CONTROL YOUR LIFE

Many entrepreneurs want control of their lives above all. Some want to work 14 hours a day while others 4 hours a day. There are those who want to stay put and not move. For whatever reasons, many entrepreneurs just want to have control of their lives.

On Xavier Roberts again. The creator of the Cabbage Patch dolls is now into stuffed animals called Furskins Bears. Xavier said,

> "I guess I'm still a kid in the way I see and the things
> I want. I don't take life too seriously and I really
> enjoy the fun things. Rich has different meanings for

different people. I wanted money to do what I want
when I want. I love to live on a grand scale."

One of the benefits and challenges as an entrepreneur is to have control
of one's life. With the benefit comes the responsibility of control, not an
easy task for everyone.

MANAGE YOUR OWN TIME

Dennis Brown obtained a law degree in South Dakota only to discover he
was not cut out to be a legal beagle. He wanted no part of the long hours,
harassing, and constant litigious haggling.

Dennis left South Dakota and drove to the West Coast. On his way, he
slept overnight at a low cost motel. His entrepreneur's mind began to turn
slowly and then more rapidly.

He tried to determine why the motel occupancy was so low. He began
to list the faults to find out that the motel was simply not catering to the
traveler. He determined that much more could be done at a minimum cost.
Low cost does not necessarily mean low service, thought Dennis. He then
notebooked the ways he could improve upon it, giving cost/benefit dollar
value to each item. (Note that Dennis had no knowledge of the motel
business.) When Brown arrived on the West Coast, he had his plan well
formulated. Dennis Brown was going to start a cost competitive, high-
value service motel. It was not long before there were more than 300 in
almost all the fifty states. A few years later, the Super 8 Motels had super
earnings. A public offering of $115 million sold out quickly. Dennis
owned about 40% of the Super 8 Motels. On the flip side, Dennis went
public with Xiox, his third high tech startup. The first two ended up in the
pits and did not make it. Xiox was, at one time, a "living dead" investment
package for Brown. Dennis Brown's work ethic was his family came first,
pleasure second, and work third. His time management was according to
rigid rules he had set. Dennis would not work past 3:30 PM. He worked
five days a week. He would travel and stay away from home and family
no more than one night at a time or travel more than two days a month!
After the Initial Public Offering (IPO) provided Dennis Brown with almost
$50 million, he bought a 112-foot yacht for the entire family to enjoy.

Remember Mervin Morris (Mervyn's) one more time. It was reported he sold Mervyn's for about $300 million. He was definite about the family-first ethic right from day one. At any time during the day, a phone call from any member of the family was put through as a top priority. It could be in the middle of an important Board Meeting, but the wheels of business stopped until Mervin handled the call. Everyone understood.

GAIN RESPECT

Many entrepreneurs want to gain the respect of family, friends, and associates. They have a Maslovian need for respect and, if they are going to get it, they have to be a success.

Terry Dorman, 27, had an urge to start his own screenpainting business. He wanted to gain respect of his peers, too. His pal was interested. They talked out the deal and decided to go for it. The duo started in Terry's basement. They planned it well. It left the blocks in low gear, picked up speed slowly, and then went into overdrive. When they passed through the third gear, Terry and his buddy were going beyond $7 million in annual sales and still accelerating.

REALIZE A GNAWING AMBITION

Business theorists and seasoned consultants rap about reasons behind startups and the impelling force of Realizing a gnawing ambition. When an entrepreneur develops a gnawing ambition, he has taken the first step on the trail to success. The idea lights a smoldering fire under the entrepreneur. It drives one to distraction, sears the hide, and the startup is consuming. The budding entrepreneur cannot dawdle or mull over the pluses and minuses. It has to be an intuitive fast forward, soon.

Momentum (Big Mo) is vital for, as in a sailboat, one can change course only when under way. Without Big Mo, a boat is dead still in the water and so with the new venture. The entrepreneur has to be guarded and make certain the gnawing ambition is not an aberration or out of the line of sight. The venture target must be "right" for capacities: skills, goals, and available resources.

For as long as he could remember, Rick Hendrick had a gnawing ambition about driving and owning cars. At 14, he bought his first motor vehicle for $250. He started road racing before he qualified for a driver's license! Who would have said Rick was going to make it big in autos?

In his early twenties, he bought his first car dealership. Not long after, Hendrick had 22 auto dealerships in eight states. His annual revenues zoomed past $400 million and his net worth ran over $100 million. When Rick reached the ripe age of 36, he was deep into road racing Chevies. He had to realize this burning ambition, to support an annual $4 million Chevy habit! One of the strongest motivating forces is the demand to realize a gnawing ambition.

THE CARROT

The carrot in entrepreneurship is accomplishment more than money. Of course, in addition to that carrot of accomplishment is the fat payoff, as Rick received. The evidence overwhelmingly posits that more than 80% of entrepreneurs were not primarily motivated by the greenback. The thrust is, far and away, the strong stimulant of accomplishment. The cash register is the way to keep score, that is for sure. But only if we chase the carrot of accomplishment with vigor will the register tinkle loud.

Bill Baker had to earn his college degree the hard way. When he graduated, he was disappointed when he could not land a good job. Not only was he not getting callbacks from job interviews, his wallet was parched.

All Baker wanted was to do a job well and make enough money to start his own company. He moved into a one-bedroom Sausalito condo. He tinkered and puttered with his ham radio hobby at night. During the day, he was deep into software programming. Bill had made a sizable fortune before he hit 25! Bill noted,

> "It seems like everyone is searching for an easy answer. But there's no answer other than believing in something and being willing to work hard and smart."

He sold his first company, Information Unlimited Software, for about $10 million. He also presided over Island Graphics Corporation of Sausalito. Bill's carrot was accomplishment, his enabling strength,

"Imagination is the key."

SOME WHO KNEW WHY

1. There was Phil Wilber, who had a good, not plush, job as vice president of a drug firm. Conventional wisdom held that drug stores could only make money selling products with high price markups. Phil disagreed and came up with a different idea—lower margins would stimulate sales to more profit! When his Board would not approve such a diverse plan, it was time to leave. He knew why. The idea was great. If they would not do it, he would! He began Drug Emporium by cutting gross margins to 20% over the cost of goods. That was 30% lower than competition and 40% lower than conventionally-priced drug stores. The Drug Emporium was a successful venture and Phil Wilber knew why.

2. Mark Leslie left Data General after eight years. He knew why. He wanted to have his own business and run it his way. He knew he would focus on his personal management philosophy. At 28 years of age, Mark started Synapse Computer in Miliptas, California. Not long after, the company took off and was flying high.

3. At Tootsie Roll candy, Ellen Gordon and Melvin Gordon knew why their company could not miss. They relied on two customer factors; quality and service. CEO Gordon asserted,

> "There are two major elements of which we never lose sight. These are *high product quality* and *assured availability.*"

They are successful and know why.

4. Michael Healy bought the family-owned Walter Brewing Company in Eau Claire, Wisconsin. Mike broke just about every good judgment rule in the good book and a few which were too basic to mention. Before he closed the deal, he consulted beer experts. After looking it over, they told him to forget the project. It was a cutthroat business and he had no experience. All Mike knew about suds was a fond memory of pretzels and his dad's tavern on the West side of Chicago. They gave sound advice. But Mike did not hear. He said,

> "I wanted to buy a small regional brewery to com-
> pete with the higher-priced imported beers. Import
> sales were growing 18% a year. The market was
> telling me something the rest of the industry ig-
> nored."

Mike knew why he could do it. In his mind, the brewery was a classic business problem opportunity. He knew that, in every problem, rests an opportunity. He had to take a crack at it because he knew he could make the brewery profitable, no matter what the experts said. Healy went full bore. The Brewery was purchased for a million dollars with the help of the Small Business Administration loan. He found it all followed Murphy's Law,

> "Nothing is as easy as it looks, everything takes
> longer than you expect, and, if anything can go
> wrong, it will, at the worst possible moment."

He ran headlong into difficulties and a nearby college business class did a financial and market study for him. Their recommendation was the brewery should be shut down. Mike nodded and kept butting his head against the wall. He believed that "triumph" is a matter of "oomph" added to "try." His perseverance paid off. He tripled the revenues and began distribution in three states. It turned out to be a remarkable startup and Mike Healy knew why.

5. After just over one year, the outspoken and flambouyant George Morrow's 16-bit laptop Pivot II computer landed on the business honor roll. The Pivot II beat out IBM's 16-bit computer for an enviable $27 million contract to supply the IRS with 15,000 laptop computers for agents. Unfortunately, a lack of cash did him in. His cash-strapped company could not hack it. George filed for protection under the Chapter XI Bankruptcy Law. He knew why he stumbled,

> "I was too much of a one-man band."

Within a week, Morrow formed a new company in Palo Alto, California, with modified expectations. He knew why he would be able to make it this time around. He kept his mistakes etched in his mind. He would not be an equity miser. He would learn to share with others. No more of the past

boo-boo of being a one-man band. He would constantly pump himself with the importance of low debt and forget pyramiding, that dangerous form of leveraging to the hilt. He would plan more rationally for rapid growth.
George said,

> "I got a 'D' on my last attempt. I'm looking for a 'B'
> or an 'A' this time."

7. Charles Winton was the early-thirties president of the Publisher's Group West (PGW) in Emeryville, California. Stated in 1976, Charles and his buddies purchased PGW for about $6,000 of debt. His story sounded like a chapter out of a how-to-do-it book merchandised by his firm, a major distributor for small and independent presses. By putting a sales force in the field to call on booksellers all over the country, the firm offered small presses and self-publishing authors entry to a national market. His niche was well focused. He would service small presses that lacked enough titles, to land a distribution agreement with a New York Publisher. Charles and his partners own 85% of the firm. The balance is distributed among employees. He says,

> "Our technique here is to sell them to the stores at a
> deep discount. It's a strategy we like because it
> encourages the book stores to merchandise the
> books."

8. Leo Lauzen was 26 when he launched his fledgling accounting business with $60 borrowed from his Rumanian mother. She wanted him to become a priest, but relented. His accounting business grew. His efforts to sell his accounting services led him to franchising his services for small firms doing less than $300,000 a year. Lauzen's mini-accounting service for small business, based in Aurora, Illinois, sold 425 franchises throughout the United States. It was soon serving more than 23,000 clients and had revenues of $40 million annually. Leo had discovered a small business niche that had largely been ignored and unfilled. Lauzen then fell in love with a purple Cadillac, the rich color of royalty. He was able to buy the purple Cadillac he loved, only to learn he had little time to drive it!

9. Howard Leendertsen was a college dropout. He started in the business world as a clothing salesman. After several small ventures, he learned of

a tanning machine which would allow even, rich bronzing without burning. Howard entered the tanning equipment business. He parlayed a loan of $12,000 into $67,500. Then he launched SCA of Redmond, Washington in 1981. Seattle was the site of his first solarium. Within the first month, business was brisk. About 140 persons went through the solarium tanning process daily.

Not long after, tanning sales grew to $30.3 million a year with a compounded growth rate of 414%! Leendertsen had 244 employees, 12 regional offices, and two quality control centers. Howard allowed as how his solarium company was the fastest growing startup in America. He knows why,

> "We are functioning in a look-good, feel-good era.
> Anything relating to vanity and health has a chance
> of being a very good enterprise."

For tanning aficionados, the Wolff Tanning facilities meant an inexpensive haven for a luscious, bronze tan. For Howard Leendertsen, it meant a golden glow.

10. Rambunctious Michael Wayne had a goal, to be a millionaire before he hit 40. In his mind, one thing was sure, he was not going to make it as a marketing manager for IBM. He had always wanted to be an entrepreneur. Mike decided to start a company to make plastic liners for pickup trucks, though, "At the time, I didn't know anyone who owned a pickup!" He saw a niche that was available to anyone. He filled it and made a fortune. At age 39, the stock offering made him a multi-millionaire worth at least $25.5 million! It was a long way from his first job as a newsboy delivering papers.

What they all prove is there is no lack of opportunities or new venture spirit in people. Entrepreneurs know the American Dream is out there, well and happy, just waiting for those with enough drive, determination, and chutzpah to grab the opportunity baton and run with it. The problems and challenges are enormous. Why be an entrepreneur to attempt to scale the heights? It is a great and exhilerating experience in which there appear to be no limits.

Michael Korda wrote,

> "The American dream is not dead. Opportunities are

> still available, and the ability to see and exploit them
> is as rewarding as ever."

So do it if you have a mind to!

W. Clement Stone says that one should have a definiteness of purpose, a positive mental attitude, a mastermind networking alliance, accurate thinking, and controlled attention: then get on with it.

SOME COMMON MYTHS

> Entrepreneurship means having the right answers. Being boss is a wonderful goal. Entrepreneurship is not crap shooting. A product can create a market. Entrepreneurship means following the rules. To make mistakes is to be defeated. Entrepreneurship means not being ambiguous. Luck and timing are controllable. Entrepreneurship and creativity cannot be learned. If it ain't broke, don't fix it. Entrepreneurship and innovation are predictable.

SOME UNCOMMON TRUTHS

1. Entrepreneurship IS the way to a fulfillment. (It is also a way for a desired monetary outcome.)
2. Being the boss is DEMANDING, DIFFICULT, AND LONESOME. (But it allows one to control one's destiny.)
3. There is NO certainty for the entrepreneur. (Stephen King might have written the script. So what.)
4. Entrepreneurship is TOTAL commitment! (Anyone who believes differently, should stay out.)
5. Entrepreneurs have LITTLE control over the future. (It is being able to react quickly to happenings.)
6. MARKET DEMAND is more than just need. (Without a MARKET DEMAND, the product is suboptimized.)
7. Entrepreneurs SHOULD let go gracefully. (They are best suited for the startup phase only.)

8. Entrepreneurs are ANYBODYS. (Loners, introverts, interactors, and gregarious.)
9. Entrepreneurship is NEVER orderly or predictable. (Expect the unexpected, constantly.)
10. There is always more than one way to do things. (No cookie cutter pattern will fit every situation.)
11. Entrepreneurship is the ability to create and build. (It is a human and creative and fulfilling act.)
12. ANYONE can become an entrepreneur. (But one must get off the pot.)

When asked why he climbed Mount Everest, Sir Hilary said, "Because it was there." That is reason enough. Why become an entrepreneur? Because it is there, for the taking.

4
HOW TO BECOME AN ENTREPRENEUR

THE MANY TYPES OF ENTREPRENEUR

In understanding how to become an entrepreneur, the words entrepreneurs should live by are,

"Do what you love and love what you do."

Sir William Osler aptly wrote:

"Find your way into work in which there is an enjoyment of it, and all shadows of annoyance seem to flee away."

The road to success for an entrepreneur is not clearly marked and never was. There are no footprints to follow with certainty, no surefire solution, and no guarantees. There is only probability and that should be good enough. First off, we must know us. We should do an inventory of our strengths and weaknesses. After that self appraisal, we identify types of entrepreneurs. Once the mirror view is completed, we know the kind of entrepreneur we are, the niche is clearly scoped, and we match our skills in the niche. That strategy has optimized our positioning. Now we can make a commitment and go for it! That is how to become an entrepreneur. It is in the proper balancing of all of those factors with unique answers which will lead to the high road. It is all possible to do it all systematically and it works wonders!

Jesus, in the Book of Matthew was right on:

> "Ask, and it shall be given you; seek and ye shall
> find; knock, and it shall be opened unto you."

There are many types of entrepreneurs:

Team Player

There are two most-used kinds of Team Players startups. One is when three or four form a startup team. Each becomes a team player with a needed skill to bring to the table. One person is the entrepreneur and leader. Two to four team players frequently join together in a startup, rarely more. A multiple team of more than one serves many sound purposes.

Team players may help in the following ways:

- lessen the workload;
- provide needed interaction;
- make consensual contributions;
- reduce individual risk;
- share the personal financial exposure; and
- are necessary for venture funding.

Occasionally, a lone entrepreneur will initiate the startup. This might occur when funding is not a major issue, the startup can be bootstrapped, or venture money is available. The entrepreneur may bring team players on board as the startup passes through stages. A second type of team player starts a franchise, where the venture is the shadow of a successful startup. In this case, the entrepreneur joins a franchise group, pays a fee for entry and training. A small commission is charged on gross revenues, for which guidance and supporting services are provided. The advantage of franchise team playing is to lessen danger and pitfalls. It is a more stable form of a startup, with less surprises. It is typically easier to manage, to finance, and has proven guidelines for managing. The probability of reasonable profitability, though modest, is enhanced with the clear footprints of a franchise. Entrepreneurs have started out as team players in franchises and, having learned the procedure of growing a new venture, have gone off on their own on another. One must remember, the gains of franchise startups are not as spectacular as non-franchise new ventures. The losses are also not as devastating. That is not always the case, but the difference between the pure entrepreneur team playing and the franchise team playing is trading off pain (risk) for gain (success). The amount of risk assumed, in the team player concept, does not change from any other startup. It is a direct proportion tradeoff. If risk is great, potential gains are great. When risk is small, potential gains are small. There is no free handout! Some entrepreneurs will band together, in small segments to replicate a franchising scheme. There can be a synergism and it often works well.

Jonathan Rosenthal, at 29 years of age, was an advocate of the Team Player concept. Deregulation had cut airline service out to about 50% of the airports in the U.S. Flights to others were reduced severely.

"Rosie" started NetAir International. NetAir International developed an air taxi service team-type group. This was a strategy to effectively serve peripheral airports. His plan was to establish a network of charter aircraft in all sizes, from small propeller aircraft to luxury business jets. It better suited passengers in speed, convenience, and overall travel flexibility. This target group of travelers were not price sensitive. He formed 4000 air taxi operators into the national air charter network team.

Inventor

Being an Inventor gives a proprietary competitive leg up. Inventors typically invent first-time products, not derivatives. When they do, if it is a successful invention, there is a significant competitive advantage. Inventor entrepreneurs have proven that lacking a business background is NOT a shutoff requirement in launching a new venture. Twenty percent of no prior business experience startups by inventors have been successful. Another paradigm is:

Lack of business experience is not a roadblock.

Many successful inventor entrepreneurs had no business backgrounds. Cases in point are Devlin, Osborne, Land, Lear, Edison, Amdahl, and a host of others. After a product has been invented and developed, there are business setup consultants who can lead the inventor, by the hand, through the startup process. It just means the road will be a little rougher.

The scientific pocket calculator, HP-35, was conceptualized by Bill Hewlett. Experienced market researchers were almost unanimous in a doom and gloom prediction the HP-35 would fall flat. William Hewlett and intuitive David Packard believed otherwise. With no business experience in this field Hewlett and Packard started HP to manufacture, produce, and sell the HP-35. The HP gizmo proved to be the death of the slide rule! If we look at statistics, about 80% of all new ventures are derivatives of former products. The Boeing 737 has gone through the -100, -200, -300, -400- and the -500 derivatives. Steve Jobs' NeXT computer is an assemblage of present technology in a unique way to develop a synergy and a super computer. In that regard, inventing may be putting together existing technology in a way not done before.

Nicher

As markets expand, small niches develop which will support a product specifically designed for that small crevice. Often the niche market is not large enough for a company. The Nicher will develop a product which fits snugly in the small-time segment. The most-followed and successful strategy is followed to maintain a low profile, so as not to awaken the sleeping market giants.

K. Philip Hwang arrived in the U.S. with $59 in his pocket.

He set out immediately and found a job. He worked hard and squirreled away money. One day, he chanced upon a televideo market niche. Hwang took his life savings and gambled to launch a on his product which fit that niche like a wet T shirt. Hwang maintained a low profile, moving low and slow in the beginning, until well established. In 1975, his niche company came awake and went public. Hwang's stock was valued at $610 million!

Exploiter

Exploiting a market segment opportunity is the ballgame. The opportunity itself does not, and never will, make a new venture successful. It is how the opportunity is exploited that scores the most runs. Entrepreneur consultants are nodding groupies in their conviction it is better to have an "A" exploiting team on a "B" opportunity than a "B" exploiting team on an "A" opportunity. Exploiting may be enhanced with experience, but experience will not compensate for a lack of willingness to exploit. Exploiters are doers, flat out. They are pivotal to the success of a startup. They are evangelical about the venture; unwavering, pumped up, and heroes on the march to the beat of seventy-six trombones. If the opportunity languishes on the drawing board, it gathers dust, nothing more. It must be exploited effectively! On the other hand, should the startup be exploited poorly, it will be an exercise in futility. Exploiting cannot be taught; it can only be learned.

The key to success of any startup is:

The strategic exploitation of an opportunity.

There must be an exploiter in every startup!

Builder

The Builder will build on a concept which has a long way to go. The Builder also thrives on incremental and positive growth. It is said of the Builder that they can be extremely patient and also impatient.

Al Paulson was a winged Builder of the first class. He was an Iowa farm boy who became a TWA Flight Engineer. One day he bought four surplus prop-driven engines from Constellation aircraft and tried to sell them to TWA. "Go back to the flight deck, Al," he was told. "Our need is for parts, not engines." Al returned to his shop. He put on his coveralls, tore down all four engines, and sold the parts for several times more than he had offered the engines! From that bitty whelping, entrepreneur Al Paulson built an aviation empire. He began wheeling and dealing in surplus aircraft, engines, and spares. He acquired small aviation-related companies. Paulson bought Grumman's business aircraft division as well as the Aero Commander aircraft and facilities. He continued buying and building. Not long after, Al Paulson, Builder extraordinaire, unloaded his sprawling aviation empire to Chrysler. His holdings were worth $550 million. Later on, Chrysler decided they wanted to remain in the automobile business only. They sold it back to an investment group headed by Paulson. Al used investment bankers' funding for this go-around.

Intrapreneur

The Intrapreneur functions within the sheltered wing of a corporation, as has been discussed. The concept has not been beaten to death and it is worthy of yet another small discussion. Persons within companies often discover niche opportunities and recommend jumping on it to exploit the segment. Some parent firms elect to bankroll an Intrapreneur rather than let the idea and the person, slip through corporate fingers even if the niche is small, provided it shows growth potential. Most companies recognize the value of a key employee. There is also the danger the key employee will leave and start a company to fill the market segment. The new venture is funded by the company and the majority stockholder is the parent company. The Intrapreneur then becomes an Entrepreneur still on the payroll of the parent corporation.

Why does this happen?

1. The segment might not be large enough to meet corporate goals but it can provide a barrier to entry.
2. If the market has growth promise, this is one way to be established in the market when it becomes robust enough.
3. It might utilize idle resources.
4. If labor relations are under strife, it might be a good strategy to launch a non-union new firm.
5. An intrapreneurial venture may also fit the long range goals and objectives of the firm.
6. Such a venture has a lower rate of risk of failure because the corporation is familiar with:

   • The market,
   • The personnel,
   • Has resources to last.

This assumes that the product fits in with the corporate marketing resources. The Intrapreneurial innovation process is less proactive than the exploiter's process. The Intrapreneurial strategy works well for many firms and is often an excellent vehicle for reluctant Entrepreneurs who want startup experience without going for broke or going broke.

Stephen Berkley recalls when his form, Quantum, took advantage of an emerging market niche opportunity. Quantum top management decided to spin off an independent subsidiary to develop a low-cost, add-on board for increasing storage in personal computers. The niche was clearly identified. The company ponied up $4 million in seed money, keeping 80% ownership in their saddlebag. The new firm, PLUS, distributed the remaining 20% of the shares among Intrapreneur Berkley and key employees.

Turnarounder

Whereas the Turnarounder might not seem like an Entrepreneur type, they are because they typically start from square one or minus one. Turnarounders are called in when a startup falters. They are hatchetpersons. Their objective is to save a corporate life by reversing a negative cash flow and to apply CPR (Cash, Planning, and Resources). They are ruthless, focused on one task: to save a new venture from going down the tubes. Turnarounding is a particular talent and a track record supports the contention. It is a specific skill. The Turnarounder also enjoys bountiful fruits of labor; an excellent salary with perks, huge stock options, and an oversized performance nosegay.

Some time ago, Memorex was down on its knees with a negative net worth, which was getting worse. It had a horrendous negative cash flow. Turnarounder Robert Wilson was brought in by the Bank of America. Wilson had an incredible turnaround record at Collins Radio among others. The millions of dollars used to entice Wilson and the millions in stock options were well worth it to the debt holding Bank and the shareholders. The double digit millions of annual losses were soon turned around into double digit millions in annual profit!

Turnarounds can also evolve an unsual scenario. When Carl Icahn raided TWA and began a successful turnaround, if not miraculous, he was so enchanted with the airline, he kept it. It became a cash cow for Icahn.

Turnarounder Victor Kiam fell in love with the deeply-troubled Remington Shaver Company. So he bought it. The recovery was dramatic. His $4 million investment came back to him quickly and much more.

Kiam's message is that,

> Turnaround is 80% hard work, 10% luck, and 10% timing.

There are four types of startups.

1. High Tech. This is in fields such as computers, software, lasers, fiber optics, robotics, bio-genetics, and the like. As many as 80% of startups in the Silicon Valley are High Tech. The High Tech entrepreneur is typically larded with impressive engineering credentials. Extensive Research and Development takes place before a product is Alpha or Beta tested.

Mike Devlin and Paul Levy attended the Air Force Academy as engineering students in the same class. After graduating one and two in their class, they were assigned to Moffett Field in California. On their off time, Devlin designed both hardware and software applications specifically for the defense industry. Paul Levy refinanced his condo. Rational Machines Inc. (RMI) was founded. Not long after, Lockheed bought a piece of the action for $10 million. Then IBM became a major joint venturer. The company appears to be turning into another one of VC Arthur Rock's incredible money machines. Mike and Paul recently crossed the 30-year old marker!

George Hara, a high tech entrepreneur, started Gekee, a laser application for use in outdoor advertising. He was able to get the company up and running, then sold it to Disney in Japan. Hara is now back in the Silicon Valley as a venture capitalist.

2. Low Tech. In this startup, the product and/or the process is not in high technology. Ski equipment, jogging accessories, multi-speed bikes, Toys-R-Us, quartz watches, Ralph Lauren's Polo, and such fit into this category.

Martin Himmel pocketted his first million selling expensive Zizanie men's cologne to Faberge in 1971. He then formed a health-and-beauty aids firm. Martin recently let go of $27.7 million worth of his $130 million stock holdings. Next on Martin's agenda? Martin's hobby is his work. His dreams are ever soaring above Cloud 9. It will not be long before Martin Himmel will have another venture on the roll. New ventures and success go together for him like bagel and lox.

What makes Roy Thorpe such a success? He had an education at MIT, for one reason. Then he taught himself creative problem-solving techniques. Roy is president of American Rail Tours. His dad taught him the rudiments of entrepreneurship,

> "My father owned a small business and taught me that, if you bought something for a dollar, you had to sell it for two or three."

It was in 1973 that he got the bug to buy a private rail car and started Falcon Safety Products, Inc. He is into manufacturing and railcars and is a millionaire, at least.

3. No Tech. It turns out that this process is simple as cottage industries where products can be made at home. No technical skill and little training is necessary.

Brett Johnson, 25, was an economics major at Harvard. He bought a batch of peaked cotton caps for $1 apiece, stamped them with a crimson "H" and sold them for $2.50 at the Harvard-Yale football game. With that profit and $1500 borrowed from his grandmother, Brett organized Crowd Caps. Annual revenues soon exceeded $15 million.

4. Service. A business without a product qualifies as a service. About 20–30% of all startups fall into the service industry. The number of service startups is increasing at a faster rate than technology new ventures. Advertising, producing plays, cleaning services, executive search, investment companies, insurance, real estate, all come to mind.

Yale Brozen was 22 and a sophomore at Columbia University. He took a summer job with a New York travel agency. From his summer experience, he decided not to return to school. He struck out on his own as a specialist of cheap flights to Europe. Hand holding with airlines and charter companies gave him access to deeply-discounted fares to fill unoccupied aircraft seats. An empty airline seat cannot be inventoried to be sold later. It is the bane of airline yield managers. Yale's company, Access International, has offices in New York and Paris. Annual revenues top $5 million.

There is a high probability way to success in service startups, a low probability way, and a no way, Jose.

In just a few years Manufactured Homes Inc's sales reached $120 million with a compound annual growth rate of 100%! President Bob Saul confided,

> "The secrets to success are so damn simple that
> people just don't see 'em."

How to become a successful entrepreneur

Self appraisal. It all starts with a self appraisal which should be done in a quiet environment. Make a realistic appraisal of personal resources, finances, experience, strengths, goals, weaknesses, and wants out of life. Then it must be read, audited, reread, and edited. After several swipes, the appraisal will be a reasonable internal appraisal. A judgement can be made as to whether the new venture dovetails with what the entrepreneur has to offer. It will reinforce beliefs where there is an entrepreneurial match. A personal balance sheet will prescribe available resources, draw guidelines, and eliminate startup choices that might develop into disasters. The primary function of the self appraisal is to prevent going beyond one's reach. To take on a startup project in excess of financial, mental, or physical resources is a dumb-dumb from the start. It is a no-win situation.

A supporting paradigm is:

> "It is more important to start a *right* new venture
> than to start a new venture *right*."

Examples of mismatched startups might be developing a new heart transplant system or starting an international airline. Dom De Luise wanting to be a high hurdler is another. Dudley Moore had better not try out for the Lakers basketball team. Small man Hervé of Fantasy Island should never get in the ring with a sumo wrestler. It is important for the entrepreneur to know the demands of a startup and how that matches the entrepreneur's experience, expectations, and skills. The three characteristics of successful entrepreneurs are:

1. Motivation
2. Commitment
3. Focus

Most entrepreneurs who made it had Motivation to the eyeballs; Commitment to the hilt; and had a clear Focus on the target.

1. Motivation is an all-out concept with:

   - the push-to-shove drive;
   - full forward overdrive all of the time;
   - a booster rocket up for every stage, and
   - a touch of old time evangelical class.

2. Commitment is unswerving dedication to the new venture:

   - the conviction that this is it, nothing else;
   - being shot out of a cannon, no change, no slow down, and no heading alterations;
   - single-mindedness;
   - knowing long hours and lost weekends are A-OK; and
   - past the point of no return from day one

3. Focus is an eye on one target:

   - every day, hour, and moment focused on another;
   - blinders as SOP (Standard Operating Procedure); and
   - enticing distractions are ignored.

Never mind that you know some who made it without Motivation, Commitment, or Focus. Some bumbled into the center ring of success by the purest of chance, and that scenario is not worth duplicating.
Let us look at this Matrix:

SUCCESS

		LOW	HIGH
PLANNING	HIGH	UNLIKELY	BINGO!
	LOW	ZILCH!	HARD WAY

IMPLEMENTATION

It is a rare entrepreneur bird that possesses all three characteristics, at all, or in equal proportions. The burning question is, can one get "characteristic user friendly"? Why Not? Are all three necessary? Desirable. Are they Learnable? Yes. Is it difficult? No!

To some degree, each of these characteristics can be learned. In all cases they are signposts leading the way to the shortest distance between two points, Startup and Success. With these characteristics ensconced in the entrepreneur's hip pocket, it is like having Etak, that computerized road map available for cars. All the driver has to do is follow directions. Trailing the computer display road signs is a breeze. They are plain to read, in understandable language, and the moving pip on the screen is reassuring evidence of on course. We are marking a simplicity pattern to success. Of course the rest is up to the cutter. This is a fast ball chest high over the outside corner of the plate. It is the chestnut that pitchers try to avoid throwing for it is a grand slammer in the making. In the final analysis, however, the batter has to make it happen! Often, budding entrepreneurs come up with slam bang ideas. They roam around restlessly, and kick the dirt, because they have a good job, satisfactory working conditions, and a healthy paycheck coming in regularly. They are stymied. They may not be motivated to break loose of the safety line and take the gamble. They simply are not motivated to trade their security blanket for the turmoil of unpredictable entrepreneurial life.

When a startup called Robotics was ready to go, one partner wanted to remain in his job until the R&D jelled and there was more assurance that the project was a go. The partner was not prepared to commit and that is mandatory. He wanted to play it safe. Financing was not available under those conditions because commitment is necessary.

Consider the entrepreneur who developed a unique transfer switch for computers that allowed multiple printers to be used with a flick of a switch selector. It was a simple product with a wide market demand. Sales were robust. A major hardware manufacturer offered it as optional accessory equipment. The entrepreneur was so charged with success of the switch, he developed multiple vision. He began developing more and more innovative products. His focus went ape. Within a year, he had more than fifty new products in his skunk works. He wanted to repeat his earlier success more than fifty times. Competitive predators snuck into the primary switch market and trouble began. Soon the positive cash flow went negative. The company began to bleed off the cash reserves. Then the negative cash flow became a ruptured aorta. Investors' protests fell on deaf ears. Within two years, the company was at the money dregs. The venture capitalists had to step in and take charge. They relieved the founder of his job. But only after the management committee physically evicted the founder from the company did they put in additional funds. The venture capitalists and other investors took over management.

Focus was re-established. Almost all of the new products were put on hold. In less than six months the company was making tracks with a modest positive cash flow! Losing focus was disasterous!

It takes Motivation, Commitment, and Focus to start a new venture.

FORMS

The entrepreneur has several business form options available. It is important to look for a fit, carefully determining which one will affect personalities, profit, taxes, growth, and resources to meet the challenges of the marketplace.

There are four legal forms:

- Sole Proprietorship
- Partnership
- Corporation
- Public Company

Each of the basic business forms becomes a little more complicated. There are many variations. No business organization form is permanent.

Most startups begin as the easy-to-do Sole Proprietorships.

The business later moves up the scale as changes occur, its operation, and needs vary. Financial ramifications and tax consequences will alter the way the business must be conducted. Therefore, the entrepreneur must re-examine the business framework at regular intervals or when dramatic changes occur, to ensure the most suitable business form.

Sole Proprietorship

In this simple form, the entrepreneur is the sole proprietor and owner. This means absolute control of the company.

Advantages:

1. Easy to form and dissolve
2. Minimum capital needed
3. Complete control
4. Keep all of the profits
5. Tax benefits and writeoffs
6. Rapid decision-making
7. Ability to make long term decisions
8. Do not have to answer to anyone

Disadvantages:

1. Personal liability may be extensive
2. Only one internal capital source
3. Difficult to maintain continuity
4. Size is limited
5. Entrepreneur is lone motivator and leader
6. Must look in the mirror to make decisions

Partnership

This is an association of two or more persons to operate a business for profit as joint owners.

The Partnership is often the second step and form that a new venture takes. It is usually created by an agreement or contract between owners which describe the duties, responsibilities, and obligations of each of the partners. Unfortunately, the law does not recognize partnerships as a legal entity, but rather as a number of individuals (sole proprietors) involved in a business. In the matter of two persons, the assets and debts belong to both partners.

Either can be called upon for full payment!

That means that either partner can go out and debt burden the company without permission. The partner with the money is usually the financial goat.

Advantages:

1. Easy to form
2. Small amount of capital needed
3. More capital available
4. Management base is larger
5. Continuity is better controlled
6. Satisfactory as long as partners are friends

Disadvantages:

1. Unlimited liability
2. Divided authority
3. May have discontinuity
4. Capital limitations
5. Size restrictions
6. Difficult time when arguments occur

There are also limited partnerships. In this case, the Limited partners are liable for the amount of their investment while the General partner is wholly liable. That is a simplistic description, necessitating research as interpretations vary, laws change, and the variations are numerous. There is also the Subchapter-*S* corporation. It is a pass through entity. About 50% of corporations are Subchapter-*S*. It has distinct tax shelter considerations for some investors who want limited liability.

Advantages:

1. Generally, an *S* Corporation pays no taxes
2. Shareholders pay taxes on all earnings at their individual rate, usually lower than the corporate rate
3. Limited liability as a standard *C* corporation
4. Behaves like a corporation

Disadvantages:

1. Cannot have more than 35 shareholders
2. Permits one class of stock
3. Cannot own 80% or more of another company
4. Shareholders must pay income tax on earnings whether they are distributed or retained by the company for working capital

5. Shareholders might be stuck with a large tax bill with no cash to pay for it
6. Banks often add loan covenants to restrict distribution of earnings to shareholders
7. There can be federal tax liabilities for everyone, if not paid

Corporation

A Corporation is an association of individuals and has a separate legal form. It is recognized legally as having an existence detached from the individuals who own it.

Advantages:

1. Limited liability
2. Separate legal entity
3. Ownership can be transferred
4. Management can be specialized
5. Continuous existence
6. Accommodates a large size well
7. Expansion is simple
8. Easy to raise capital

Disadvantages:

1. Regulated closely
2. Taxation is specific
3. Charter restrictions
4. Expensive to organize
5. Public disclosure
6. Difficult to obtain credit
7. Shareholders may limit flexibility

Public Company

Publicly held companies have stockholders and are governed by the rules of the Security Exchange Commission (SEC). The shares are traded on the open market and public reporting is essential.

Advantages:

1. It is possible to sell Founders' stock under most circumstances
2. Large sums of money are available
3. Shareholders may be a customer base
4. Stock price gives performance cues
5. Expansion is less difficult
6. Banking relationships are better

Disadvantages:

1. Shareholder responsibility
2. Public disclosure
3. Government regulations limit mobility
4. Costs a great deal of money
5. Long term goals harder to implement

The laws of various states influence the characteristics of the forms of business organizations.

> An attorney should be consulted prior to making a decision on the intial business structure and at every change.

Tricks of the trade:
Get a mindset. Always be a Dreamer.
  Take thirty minutes each day in a quiet nook.
  Make this the creative think time.
  Is this what I really want?
  Where am I going?
Set goals. Reasonable Ones and Unreasonable Ones.
  Write down goals, particularly those which appear to be difficult.
  If they seem awesome, break the goals down into smaller milestones
    which can be accomplished.
  Smell the roses.
Control Your Mind.
  Practice autosuggestion and meditation on a regular basis.
  Tolerate no negative thoughts, all upbeat.
  Make your mind a bright and shining place.
  It will be a great day! Say it often!

It will happen!

Fortify. Strengthen.

Fortify your mind by sending out positive suggestions to influence events.

Memorize quotations that are stimulating and meaningful.

Repeat them often. They will become internalized.

They will be driven from your conscious into your subconscious mind and fortify you.

Keep an Open Mind—Wide Open.

Keep your mind ajar. Be on the lookout for new ways of entrepreneurship.

Read and use self-help books, all tools.

Listen to motivational audio tapes and watch visual tapes.

Attend inspirational lectures.

Imagine. Visualize.

Develop visual images of the step by step process and how you will gain each step.

Imagine the total project and how it will be accomplished.

See an image of it as a large success. Believe it!

What will make it happen is redundancy and reinforcement.

Remember Henry Ford's admonition that if you think you can do it or think that you cannot, you are probably right.

When it is a Go, Set Sights. Focus.

Pinpoint the goals.

Concentrate on the project.

Write down how the objectives will be achieved.

No negative thoughts, only realistic ones.

Maintain High Principles. No Compromises.

Recognize, accept, and live by all of the high principles that will help achieve good physical, mental, and moral health as well as happiness.

You are the sum total of your principles.

According to the Scriptures, "As a man thinketh, so shall he be."

Live by the Golden Rule, "Do unto others as you would have them do unto you."

Never, but never, compromise your ethical beliefs!

Network. Extend the Ganglia.

Happiness is sharing your time, expertise, wealth, dreams, knowledge, and blessings with others.

Be a good talker and a better listener, in short, an A-one communicator.
Genuinely like people and they will like you!
Measure Time. It is Pure Gold!
This is the fundamental step of thinking it out.
How much time will it take? Daily? Total?
Is this the highest and best use of time?
Am I willing to spend the time?
What does the time away from the family mean?
At my age, is the time available?
Now. Not Later!
No loitering.
Do it now!
Delays gnaw away and harass.
A journey of a thousand miles begins with a first step.
Remember to pause and let success catch up.

SOME COMMON MYTHS

1. Entrepreneurs do not have to be planners.
2. Entrepreneurs are obedient and compliant.
3. It can be done alone.
4. The product is the all.
5. Supply can create demand.
6. Extended research will guarantee success.
7. Be careful, conservative, and safe.
8. Being entrepreneurial is a 40-hour week.
9. Spend money in anticipation of growth for facilities, equipment, and personnel.
10. The first smash is a guarantee of a second.

SOME UNCOMMON THOUGHTS OF SUCCESSFUL ENTREPRENEURS

1. You become the goal you think of most.
2. If it is to be, it is up to you.
3. Dare and you will accomplish, in proportion.
4. You cannot make it uphill if you think downhill.

5. Peak performers are those who overcome limiting beliefs and negative expectations.
6. Bend instead of break.
7. Be rebellious, there are a thousand ways.
8. Communications builds bridges, not walls.
9. Enterprises have no future, people do.
10. You are today, born yesterday, building a tomorrow.
11. Luck is when preparation meets opportunity.
12. In every crisis is a win-win somewhere.
13. If data are still available, it is too late.
14. Enter muddied, uncertain markets; if there is clarity, someone else is there.

So how does one get started? First, a self appraisal. Who are you? What do you want? Are you willing to commit? Then try the idea on friends for size letting the enthusiasm, confidence, and jabber flow. The next step is to get a team together, a miniplan verbalized, and launch. All parties must be on the same wavelength. The next step is to get a plan written for the startup.

Then, take off and go for it! Money is the fuel and that is a difficult task. Be sure that there is enough to do the job! That is how to! Do you want to get going? A resounding YES! Follow the roadsigns. It is easy. But get moving! You are nowhere until you get the ball rolling.

Remember Machiavelli:

> "And it ought to be remembered that there is nothing more difficult to take in hand, more perilous in its success, than to take the lead in the introduction of a new order of things. Because the innovator has for enemies all those who have done well under the old conditions, and lukewarm defenders in those who may do well under the new. This coolness arises partly from fear of the opponents . . . , and partly from the incredulity of men, who do not readily believe in new things until they have had long experience with them."

5

HOW TO BE CREATIVE

Remember Jonathan Livingston Seagull?

> "Don't worry about creativity. Just learn to fly real
> well and when you do, the magic will happen. You'll
> go beyond the barrier without realizing it."

Creativity is letting the mind soar to new heights. Do not try to define creativity. Only Steve Martin can; not make sense, but define it (with an arrow through his head). There are no cozy rules, for creativity is simply not neat.

Rudolf Flesch wrote,

> "Creative thinking may mean simply that there's no
> particular virtue in doing things the way they have
> always been done."

CREATIVITY IS MADE OF WHAT?

In the United States, unoccupied space in a warehouse is referred to as empty. The Japanese do not refer to the space as being empty. They say,

"It is full of nothing." So it is with creativity. It comes from, not necessarily obvious thoughts, but from the empty spaces between thoughts, seemingly unstructured nonthoughts. Creativity occurs on the edge of human experience and not in the midst of routine events. Creative ideas come from a potpourri of strange and unexpected geneses. They pop up by chance, made of a suggestion "Why don't they . . . ?", from someone while hanging on a cable car, bounding on a moped, jogging on the beach, chomping on a sourdough bagel, or watching David Letterman. Created ideas are occasionally so random as to appear to be in another galaxy. Yet some semblance of order is necessary for creativity requires an ability to think creatively with some direction. Notions about creativity are marvelously two-faced. Some call it the premises of the flower children, ESP by candlelight, or the Belushi occult. Others say it is an absolutely rational process. It has been written by pundits that only in mathematics can there be no true controversies. (Then a student at Cal upset one of Newton's mathematical laws unchallenged for centuries!) Perhaps it is a pelvic disorder. Who knows? To resolve its composition is not high on the priority list. The same might be said of the makeup of creativity as Supreme Court Justice Potter Stewart said of pornography. The good Justice Stewart observed,

"I can't define it, but I know it when I see it."

Creativity is probing the uncharted, speldunking without a torch and that is the way it always has been. Creativity in entrepreneurship is made of wonderful stuff. It is challenging and stimulating and bonkers and makes the entrepreneur's world so enticing. You must have enough faith to take free time and allow the valuable ideas bubble up. Intuition is to creativity what Robin is to Batman. Masked, they complement each other. Intuition is mental foreplay; feeling, smell, hunch, signal, itch, Extra Sensory Perception (ESP), psychokinesis, gut wrench, and go signals that prod. Without it, creativity is a downer. Albert Einstein saw the general theory of relativity in an intuitive vision. He created the theory and filled in the logic later! Intuition plays a prominent role during the first two startup phases. Later in the life of a new enterprise, intuition is relied on less and relegated to a tailbone position. A pervasive notion is that intuition is made up of hunch and instinct, but no one really has a handle on it. To some, Roy

Rowan, for example, "hunch" is an odious word. He describes it as a horseplayer's term rife with unpredictability and imprecision.

Roy defines hunch as:

> "Knowledge gained without rational thought (that) comes from some strata of awareness just below the conscious level."

This may sound heavy, but it is not. To others, hunch and instinct are interchangeable with intuition. It matters only that entrepreneurs rely on the right side of the brain which governs the intuitive, artistic, and creative processes. Whatever intuition is, it is the enabling factor in creativity. It may be that the ultimate gift we might be given is illusion. Remember the Hula Hoop startup? If it has been evaluated in left side logic, it would have been committed to the funny farm. The product was off the wall and did not have a prayer. There was simply not a scintilla of need or market demand, no call for anything resembling a round plastic tube to twirl around the tummy. For what? Whammo executives, long on intuition and frivolity, plunged headlong. The Hula Hoop was a phenomenal success, a celebration of the right intuitive hemisphere over the left logical side. Do not forget that "Pet Rock," a classic example of the flip side of rationality! The founder rang up over $4 million for that intuitive creation. These are not isolated examples. There are many others. They support the thesis that creativity is the lifeblood coursing through emerging entrepreneurs and intuition is the enabling plaque.

Albert Einstein again,

> "When I examine myself and my methods of thought, I come to the conclusion that the gift of fantasy has meant more to me than my talent for absorbing positive knowledge."

Yet, intuition is not to be confused with fantasy. Many say it was fantasy, not intuition, that led to an ill-fated attempt by a venture capital group to greenmail Martin Marietta, Pan American Airways to buy National Airlines, Ludwig to develop Brasilia, a European consortium to build the SST Concorde, IBM to bring out the Peanut, and Ford to produce the Edsel.

THE CREATIVE ADRENALINE

To get the adrenaline flowing, the entrepreneur must follow the first law of creativity:

> "Throw Away The Rule Book!"

Creativity is the adrenaline that starts at night or at high noon, in rain or shine, and in a windstorm or during a dead calm. Ideas pop out at unexpected times and in weird ways. That is just the way it is. It has zits, is more often messy, cluttered, uncontrolled, disorganized, ambiguous, unconventional, bumbling, bull headed, challenges tradition, capricious, playful, undisciplined, occasionally ridiculous, and so refreshing. To keep matters off center; in large, mature companies, creative persons are often perceived as oddballs and, by fellow workers, as "not good team players." The corporate halls do not often provide a haven for birthing new ideas and are not constructed for entrepreneurs. It is hostile territory.

CENTERS OF CREATIVITY

In the late Seventies, the dean of a Midwestern college eliminated the teaching of creativity to business (MBA) students on the grounds that "they would never use it anyway." Today, hundreds of courses teaching creative thinking are now available at universities. Stanford University now has multiple courses on creativity. There have been massive corporate changes throughout the world in beliefs of the value of creative thinking. On any given weekday, more than 30,000 executives grunt, groan, crow, scratch, draw pictures, and attend workshops to learn or enhance creative skills. Giant corporations are flocking to creative workshops. It is the 'est' of the corporate age. "Now let's have the 'chicken cheer,'" urges the instructor. He flaps his arms and scratches at the floor. A dozen or more executives shed their coats and vests. They stand up to follow, sometimes uneasy at first. Soon the classroom is filled with falsetto crowing that would put a henhouse to shame. Why? Such classes, led by creativity evangelists, preach the creativity gospel to corporate congregations. Seminars for executives are now common fare. Like the self-help movements of the last decade, creativity development has raised the eyebrows of skeptics and the hopes of those who did not know they could be creative.

Herman Miller, Inc. (HM) is known as one of the most creative office furniture design companies in the U.S. with sales at about half billion dollars. According to Dan Peak, here are some of the ways Herman Miller stimulates a creative culture.

1. Attempts to eliminate stress and small frustrations from the daily routine.
2. Has informal meeting places scattered throughout the Herman Miller building, creating niches with thinking alcoves with plush sofas and chairs.
3. Transferred the Research Department from the headquarters office.
4. Encourages employees to design their own offices.
5. Established a corporate culture which concentrates on being imaginative and creative.
6. Holds the belief that everyone can be creative.
7. Assures employees that creativity can be taught to those who think they are on the short end of the stick.
8. Maintains that a creative thinking environment is productive and satisfying.

HOW ARE IDEAS CREATED?

Ideas are made of pure goose bumps, a Robin Williams movie, a dollop of the bizarre, an impossible Voyager flight, and trifocal vision. They are created from the most sensible and the most frivolous thoughts: at times set aside for creative meditation, and times not set aside for creative meditation.

3M has an eleventh commandment;

"Thou Shalt Not Kill A New Product Idea."

Masking tape for two-tone car painting and Post-It notes are the result of 3M's eleventh commandment. The truly creative person cruises about, head abuzz with ideas. The creative being must be able to let the reins go allow the brain to tiptoe through the tulips, dream on a star, and launch an idea no matter how zany. And it may be for no sensible reason at all. Howard Fenster is a successful entrepreneur. On the Johnny Carson show he chortled,

"I want to get me one of everything in the world!"

That is an Entrepreneur First Class talking! He does not know where or how he will get the next idea. But his mind is wide open and his sails full. He knows no limits as to what he can accomplish. He is a dreamer par excellence. The wheres and whys will be filled in later. If we are so corsetted that we cannot permit our minds to errantly race about in aimless pursuit, we should set time aside for creative thinking.

It is as Albert Camus wrote,

"If you lack character, you need a system."

Whatever it takes, is what one ought to do. The creative mind is a muscle; develop it by pumping ideas. There should always be goofy time for "I wonder why . . . ?"

WHERE DO WE CREATE GOOD IDEAS?

They are created in bed, in the shower, or at McDonalds while boffing a Big Mac (hold the mustard). You name it! Never pass a coffee (decaf) machine or a coke (diet) machine without stopping to take a moment for wanderlusting. It can be so fruitful to meander into a park and watch the dandelions grow! A stroll along Atlantic City's Boardwalk on Easter Sunday can be hectic, but one retailer entrepreneur goes there every year. He has no set goal but knows that if he keeps his mind receptive, he will drink in ideas which will build on other ideas. For him an Easter Parade is a stroll on the Boardwalk and one of his most creative and stimulating times. The creation of ideas is not the province of any intellectual group; it is in the ballpark for anyone who wants to swing a bat. You do not have to have the mind of a Da Vinci or Jefferson to be creative. There are many Phi Beta Kappas working the bridge toll gates and many passing through. To say that ideas are best created in designated environments is patently wrong. Some allow as how farm chores are great coaxers of creativity. The famed American painter, Grant Wood, allowed,

"All the good ideas I have ever had came to me
while I was milking a cow."

Others find a subway ride as the place for creativity. Sometimes the wind tunnel sounds of a jetliner or a train's rhythm makes the creative juices flow. A. Musselman said the idea for his coaster-brake was created while speeding down a Rocky Mountain path on a runaway bicycle! The coaster-brake made millions for him. Loafing is a great way to be creative. Feel no guilt when doing nothing and not accomplishing something. Think—dream—open up. The human brain is capable of producing ideas at a remarkable rate in such diverse environments. We can think tens of thousands of thoughts a day, but we do not have access to them all because so many occur at the subconscious level. We must be opened up to nothing. Even falling asleep is a sign of the creative mind, new research has shown. At the University of Arizona, 200 college students' diaries, sleep patterns, and creativity test results were analyzed. They found that 86% of the most creative students fell asleep in 20 minutes or less while 56% of the least creative students required half an hour or longer. They also found that the more creative a person is, the more likely he or she is to use dreams for solving personal and professional problems.

The link between creativity and falling asleep quickly, according to psychology researchers Ingrid Sladeczek and George Domino, may be that both require "relinquishing conscious control and letting go of everyday, rational awareness." The research was reported in *Psychology Today* magazine.

HOW THE VALUE OF CREATIONS IS MEASURED

Not all creativity has a dollar motive. Fred Gibbons at Software Publishing will tell you that. If it is self-fulfilling, it may be enough.

Dorothy Parker, the famed humorist, was lonesome in her office. She longed for friendship and casual conversation. She posted a 3-lettered sign on her office door—MEN. She had many visitors from then on, though they stayed only a short time!

Once we create, we must tear apart the grand idea. How long will it take to develop, what is the risk, the market, and estimate both sides of success, spectacular and worst case scenarios.

Our idea should be placed in a matrix against other potential startup ideas as to cost/benefits and meaning to us.

The creation must stand tall against three principal values: one, self fulfillment; two, joy of doing; and three, economic success.

Jerry Gillies follows his favorite motto,

> "If it doesn't bring me profit, pleasure, or knowl-
> edge, it isn't worth doing."

HOW CAN A CREATION BE DEVELOPED?

Creativity must be acted upon or the flow will peter out. Goethe wrote,

> "Whatever you can do or dream you can do, begin
> it. Boldness has genius, power, and magic in it."

A window of opportunity opens for only a short time. It slams shut quickly. A gusty headwind in the face of creativity is Analysis Paralysis, not knowing when enough analysis is enough. Research can put a choke hold on creativity under the guise of reducing uncertainty. Protracted research is a copout, pure and simple.

Henry Frederic Amel observed,

> "The man who insists upon seeing with perfect
> clearness before he decides, never decides."

So many negative voices leach away at good ideas and raise doubts as to abilities to create ideas. Dissonance should be ignored. In the 1800s, after seeing Rembrandt's works, a noted art critic commented,

> "Rembrandt is not to be compared in the painting of
> character with our extraordinarily gifted English ar-
> tist, Mr. Rippingille."

Mr. Rippingille? Come on now.

The only way to get rid of the fear of falling down is with a frontal lobotomy, so forget it. It can be better overcome by positive thinking.

Henry David Thoreau said,

> "If you build castles in the air, you need not be lost;
> that is where they should be. Now put the foundation
> under them."

Bombard your mind with creative ideas, experiences, and what-ifs. Get that confident ganglia into the open and let it all hang out. That is the foundation upon which ideas are built. When an idea is created, formulate it carefully. Put it down on notepaper. An idea has a great past if it remains in the head. It is so hard to remember and so easy to forget, as an old song should go. Next, network it among friends, business acquaintances and friends. Dialogue is an inexpensive and effective market basket survey. Use it or lose it, the networking information, that is.

Remember:

Use intuition in the face of opposition and logic. Create for no apparent reason at all.

Creativity calls for free thinking. No idea is without merit. Give each one a chance.

Pump creative thinking muscles. Take the most mundane and rethink it.

Piggyback a successful creation. The better creation is the enemy of yesterday's good creation.

There is no such thing as cannot be done. The impossible takes a little bit longer!

The creator must be quixotic about the product. The leaders of the pack are visibly excited about the product and believe.

SELLING CREATIVITY

Every creation has to be sold and it is not easy. Fabulous creations have gone down the drain because they were not packaged, promoted, or sold properly. How a creation is presented can turn on or turn off the listener. Note that a good creation, whose time has come, whose niche has been found, can be always find champions. Just keep looking and trucking. As H. Ross Perot, one of the richest men in America, echoed Winston Churchill,

"Never give up, never give up, never give up!"

Remember to sell a potential investor to an idea, not an idea to a potential investor!

SOME CREATIVE ENTREPRENEURS

George De Mestral was brushing burrs out of his dog's fur. He was curious about the tenacity of the burrs and examined them under a microscope. Each tiny burr was equipped with tiny hooks that snagged the fur. A light lit. There was value hidden there, De Mestral reckoned. The Velcro fastener was created.

Ruth Handler created the Barbie Doll and co-founded the Mattel Toy Company. She was stunned when she had to undergo a mastectomy. She learned that good breast protheses did not exist. To lose a breast is a calamity for a woman, but to lose her femininity was even worse. Ruth Handler threw her creative self into the task of developing a well-fitting, natural looking artificial breast. Her firm, Nearly Me, launched a new career.

Sanford Cluett created a way to stop cloth from shrinking. Someone laughingly told him that it was worth at least $5,000,000 a year. It turned out later that the Cluett Peabody Company did make as much as that from royalties.

A Russian immigrant at 16, Lena Himmelstein, was also a creator. She believed that expectant mothers would like to dress to look less expecting. She formed the Lane Bryant Company, soon to reach sales in the multi-millions.

It has been said that a creative thinker does not evolve new ideas but rather finds new combinations of old ideas. Lane Nemeth started out her toy company in a garage. She built on creative ideas from Tupperware and Mary Kay. She staged display parties in homes and showed women how to use these toys.

From only word of mouth, Lane Nemeth's company became a billion dollar company. "I made many mistakes," she said. "I never felt I couldn't make the idea work." She did it in spades, with a piggyback creation.

Three IBM engineers created an idea of a removable disk drive. They worked on the product and found it offered enornmous storage capabilities. They offered the idea to IBM and were turned down. The trio left. They formed Iomega Corporation and developed the removable disk drive. In 1987 Iomega earned $7.81 million on $115.5 million sales.

Dr. Bob Jarvik's grades were so poor that he had to start medical school in Italy. He was a medical tinkerer, always inventing something. He formed Symbion and developed the Jarvik-7 heart. Recently he bought back the rights to a surgical stapler which he created when he was 17 years old. He has created an artificial ear and a Ventricular Assist Device (VAD). Profit is around the corner.

It has been believed that a computer simulating human reason is far in the future. Yet four scientists at MIT's Artificial Intelligence Laboratory created a design of a computer for research in simulating human reason. They formed Symbolics Inc. Today, it is a breakaway leader, earning $3.8 million on $69 million in annual sales.

A classic example of creative entrepreneur in perpetual motion is Harold Butler. Quick-think Butler cannot stop entrepreneuring any more than he can stop breathing. He goes from one startup to another in fast forward. He creates great ideas, builds rapidly, goes public, makes or loses money, and exits. Harold Butler has made fortunes and lost them; three large companies valued at $1 billion and 15 restaurant concepts. "I'm the modern version of the riverboat gambler," the 64-year-old entrepreneur says. "I've been at bat more times than Babe Ruth." Some say he is resilient, others say he has a highly developed intuition, while others call him a creative genius. He has no intention of hanging up his gear as long as there is a challenge somewhere.

A creative entrepreneur is Bill Von Meister. The 43-year-old has jump-started four firms, including Source Telecomputing Corporation, a national timesharing service that was sold to Reader's Digest Association in 1980. He has created a new startup, Prizeline Communications Corporation in Vienna, Virginia. Prizeline offers a series of interactive games played over the telephone which the caller competes for cash and prizes. His fifth one looks like an out and out winner.

SOME COMMON MYTHS

Creativity is intelligence

Studies show that creativity requires only normal intelligence and a high IQ is not an overlaying benefit. Studies suggest that the threshold for creativity is an IQ of about 120. Above 130 there seems to be little correlation between increased IQ and creativity. People with low IQ scores are more often low in creativity, Though some violate that tenet. It has been concluded that creativity does not grow in parallel with higher IQ scores. If a joss stick can make one abiding paradigm burn brightly, it is that neither a low IQ nor a high IQ is a deterrent or of great benefit in creativity. Nonintellectual traits such as personal values and personality are far more important.

Creativity is dependent on education

Not if it is meant to say formal credentials. Steven Spielberg had such poor high-school grades he could not get admitted to any major film school. Wernher von Braun created America's space program yet he was a mathematical dunce in school. Albert Einstein was so slow in school that his parents thought he was retarded. He flunked his first entrance exam! P. T. Barnum created the greatest show on earth to become a multi-millionaire. He did not make it through grade school. Nor did one of the greatest creative inventors, Thomas Edison. Leon Uris flunked English three times in high school. He quit to join the marines and then became a successful author worth millions. Education is an important adjunct to the development of creative talents but education and creativity are not necessarily interdependent. Some entrepreneurs argue that modern higher education stresses logic and that tends to squelch creativity. Some experts believe that college education—two years, peaking at four—may foster creativity. They suggest that graduate school may not be all that great in some fields because advanced study reinforces logic and perpetuates entrenched thinking. Many innovators dropped out of school altogether. The late R. Buckminster Fuller, the social theorist, and Edwin Land, who invented the Polaroid camera, did not complete their degrees at Harvard University.

Creativity cannot be learned

In his book, *Conceptual Blockbusting,* Stanford Professor James Adams contends that creativity can be taught. This thesis is supported by an overwhelming number of educators.

Recent research shows that creativity is not such an elusive quality after all, and most important, it is not difficult to develop creativity skills.

It is a feat of mental aerialists engaging the conscious and subconscious parts of the brain. It draws on knowledge, logic, imagination, dreaming, and intuition to the ability to see connections and distinctions between ideas and things. There is an advanced medical imaging technique called

Positron Emission Tomography which enables scientists to view the activity in the brain. It shows that both sides of the brain, the creative right and the logical left, flicker on and off when a person is engaged in creative thought. Creativity is an ability to use both modes of thought.

Over and over, it has been proven that creativity is not a divine gift and can be learned. That much we know. For the record, creativity cannot be dog-tagged as dependent upon education.

Creativity is limited by cultural environments

Freddie Laker, the millionaire airline operator, grew up in poverty in London. Andrew Carnegie began life as a bobbin boy in a cotton factory. His father was a poor handloom weaver. Adam Gimbel started as an immigrant backwoods pack peddler. Out of a sweltering English iron foundry came Samuel Lord, an orphan boy. Their creations, Gimbels and Lord & Taylor, became two of the most successful department store chains in the U.S. Creative people apparently do not have structured and controlled childhoods. Instead, growing up is often exposed to diversity and trauma. Strains in family life—financial ups and downs or messy divorces—are common. Many experts hold that doses of the hard life gives children the unique ability to see issues and problems from a more realistic point of view.

Creativity is logical and orderly and original

Creativity is not logical or orderly. Buckminster Fuller said he invented in a void. "I might have come up with a pair of flying slippers," he noted, "But instead, it was the geodesic dome." Creativity may not be original. Bernice Fitz-Gibbon wrote that creativeness also consists of merely tuning up what is already there. Though shoes have been worn for centuries, the left and right shoes were thought up only a little more than 100 years ago!

Franklin P. Jones notes that,

"Originality is the art of concealing your source."

Almost 80% of new products are derivatives of present technology, not new products.

Creativity is irrational thinking

There are creative persons who appear to be far out, but imbalanced traits may be extensions of a receptiveness to a wider than normal range of experiences and behavior patterns. As a rule, the creative person has an exceptionally broad and enhanced self-awareness. Creative entrepreneurs can be primitive and, also, cultured; destructive and constructive; mad yet sane, and flamboyant, at the same time, conservative. Psychologists characterize creativity as demanding unusual flexibility and fluent thinking. Entrepreneurs may appear to be irrational thinkers without being so. That may be the result of having half a dozen ideas cooking on "HI" at the same time.

Creativity is not the province of irrational thinkers.

Emotional barriers stunt creativity

It may be true that emotional barriers tend to make people less creative but there is no consistency. Bankers, staid and stable, are often extremely creative. Stress does not help. Harassed persons are not loose. The truth is that if an entrepreneur is to be an entrepreneur, a new venture will take place regardless of the surrounding garbage.

Creativity must be inspiration-driven

To the contrary, no inspiration seems to exist. The entrepreneur has to get out and do it. When a young writer asked Ernest Hemingway how one could become a writer, he replied,

> "By applying the seat of your trousers to the seat of your chair."

Sometimes entrepreneurs begin because the alternative is unacceptable. They cannot work for a large corporation. They are discontented with the existing product. They want to get out of the house! Do something while the kids are in school. The best idea that has come down the pike has smoldered just too long. It can be done . . . whenever for whatever reasons.

Creativity diminishes with age

Ray Kroc was in his fifties when McDonald's was created. Edd Carlsen took over the presidency of United Airlines at the age of fifty nine and made the carrier into the largest airline in the western world.

Colonel Saunders created Kentucky Fried Chicken in his sixties. Konrad Adenauer became the leader of Germany at the age of 69.

Michelangelo created the Pieta and St. Peter's Basilica at the age of seventy, the same age as Douglas MacArthur when he was named commander of the UN forces in Korea. Ronald Reagan was in his seventies when he was elected President of the United States. Sophocles created *Oedipus Rex* at seventy and *Electra* at eighty. *Faust* was created by Johann von Goethe between the ages of seventy-six and eighty-two. The legendary house in Arizona was created by Frank Lloyd Wright as well as the Price Tower in Oklahoma when he was in his late seventies and early eighties. George Burns created an Oscar-winning movie role at the age of eighty. Aaron Copland was still composing at eighty as was Virgil Thompson at eighty-four. Grandma Moses became a famous painter in her eighties. At eighty-five, Coco Chanel was still the creative head of her Paris Fashion house. The scientist who isolated Vitamin C, Dr. Albert Szent-Gyorgyi, is still active as a researcher at eighty-eight. That Nobel Prize winner said,

> "Creativity consists of looking at the *same* thing as everyone else and seeing something *different*."

At ninety-one Adolf Zukor was chairman of Paramount Pictures, creating pictures. At 93 the Marc Chagall was still creating paintings. George Abbott was an active creative choreographer at 100 years of age.

Not everyone is creative

Not so. Creativity is for everyone and anyone. Stanford Professor Jim Adams writes,

> " . . . for most of us, creativity is more of a dull glow than a divine spark. And the more fanning it receives, the brighter it will grow."

Everyone is and can be more creative . . . in different ways. Thinking off the wall. Challenging all assumptions. Taking screwball risks. Taking advantage of mistakes as Charles Goodyear did (and discovered the vulcanization of rubber). They do it by using the "Mind's eye" (Hamlet), not the "Eye's eye."

Some Fast Lanes to Creativity:

- Pick a friendly idea, one you like. (Product and market).
- Read everything on the subject. (Books and periodicals. Know it backwards).
- Talk with people who might be the market. (Or might not).
- Join mind expanding groups. (Startups, lectures, seminars, in the field).
- Get hands-on experience. (visit plants, markets, etc.).
- Network with other startup doers. (Experts or amateurs or spectators).
- Collar people who have made it. (Ask them how?)
- Milk the financial community for information. (Friendly banker and others).
- Break the rules. (Dare to make mistakes, learn from them).
- Dream on—intuitively, get high on challenging ideas. (What if . . . ?)
- Formulate the idea and go for it! (Let intuition roam and commitment be solid).

Two important conclusions can be drawn:

1. Creativity is broad-based. It does not mean that we can all scale Everest. It does not mean that we are limited to narrow boundaries either.

2. Creativity is a tool. That is the key word. We all have it and each can do more about it. We must develop self-confidence and a creative perspective.

Creative guru Roger Von Oech has worthy guidelines:

Have passion for what you do:

If you have several ideas, go with the one that really turns you on.
Get in touch with the people who can help you; I live and die by the
  network.
Don't give up!
Visualize yourself accomplishing goals.
Eliminate things that get in the way of action.
Don't be afraid to break rules, or to make mistakes, but learn from
  them."

In conclusion, a creative fire lies banked in everyone. Its flame can be
brought to life, to shine, and to glow. The meaning of creativity hugs the
word, potential. Create an open architecture mind in which creativity will
thrive. Be inquisitive, question everything, and figure out how in the world
everything can be done better. That is the name of the creative game. You
will find that it can be done!

> "The world is ever so fair,
> To let you and me to be free.
> Not to save the earth in one magnificent crush.
> But to create with all the cunning of our being,
> The art of making anything possible."

6

HOW TO WRITE
(AND PRESENT) A
BUSINESS PLAN

THE BUSINESS PLAN STRATEGY

The primary purpose of writing a Business Plan is to raise money. The definition of a good Business Plan is one that gets the money. The Business Plan includes and describes all areas of a new venture. A good Business Plan shows an understanding of the startup and delineates the strategy to reach profitability. Though it should be a joint effort of management, sometimes it is written by the entrepreneur alone. And if the entrepreneur is like hundreds of others, there will be a lengthy home computer session to bang out a long paean to that new product or service.

Step one for a budding mogul is,

> Get a plan.

No one has ever said that preparing a Business Plan is easy. Preparing a Business Plan is sweat labor. It requires diligence, research, and applying the seat of the pants to the seat of the chair. The writer must keep in mind the basic target:

> It is written for investors, not the entrepreneur!

A Business Plan is a necessary first step in launching a new venture for the following reasons:

1. To describe a new enterprise in a Business Plan is a great way to articulate the startup and evaluate how good the idea really is.
2. It is a linear path of what is supposed to happen, with measurable milestones and short term targets.
3. It is necessary for the development, expansion, and operation of a business.
4. When recruiting key employees: desirable potential candidates are more apt to cast their lot if they have a clear understanding of the new venture.
5. Describing the business concept and implementation gets the management team in step.
6. A well written business plan is ammunition.

> Bankers like the Business Plan. Suppliers can effectively evaluate credit accommodations with a business plan.

FORMAT OF A
TYPICAL BUSINESS PLAN

I. COVER LETTER

Date
Business name, address, and phone number
Principals

(The Cover Letter should serve as an introduction, including the reason for sending the Business Plan, and reference to any recommendations.)

II. TABLE OF CONTENTS

Chapters and subheadings

(The development of the Table of Contents is an extremely important first stage of development. This should be accomplished before any writing takes place. Although it is common to use a modular format, it runs the risk of lacking an overall thrust and sequential buildup peculiar to the startup.)

III. EXECUTIVE SUMMARY

Brief overview of the company and its plan
Description of the product or service
Market demand and strategy
Primary objectives
Short financial overview

(The most important component of a Business Plan is the Executive Summary.

A one/two page summation of the entire plan, it contains two crucial elements: what the investor is being asked to do and a clear explanation of why a customer will buy the product or service.

John Mumford, a partner at Cross Point Venture Partners in Palo Alto, said, "That has to jump out at any reader. If someone reads the executive summary and doesn't come away with that clearly fixed in his mind, the plan isn't a success."

This short section should whet the appetite of the investor reader. It is a carrot which assures the reader that it will be worthwhile to go on.)

IV. HISTORY

Background of principals and company origin
Product/service description
Current stage of development
Corporate structure
Statement of firm's success or experience

(The History section is the backdrop. In this section is the date and place, including the state of incorporation, and any other legal references of importance.

It is a recount of the new venture. How the product came into being, what the new venture is, when the idea was germinated, etc.

It should list the entrepreneurial group, founding directors, and shareholders.

There should be a discussion of important changes in the structure of the company, its management, or its ownership.

Of importance are any successes the company has had in the field up to now. If the entrepreneurs or founders have had successes, those should be noted, for experience is important.)

V. DEFINITION OF THE BUSINESS .

Principal products or services
Unique features to give a competitive advantage
Detailed annual sales for the past five years, if available
Discussion of the industry, the total market and the demand
Seasonal and cyclical observations
Maturity of the product line
Patents, trademarks, or other trade advantages such as labor or geographic or special deals

(Discussion of the industry, the total market, and the demand:

It is important to overview the industry, size, and growth. The industry must have growth! The total market is defined and also the segment which is to be exploited. The demand should be quantified and qualified.

The principal products or services should be described. Also the unique features as compared to competition.)

VI. PRODUCT/SERVICE

Competitive advantage
Description and where it is in its life cycle
Status of research and development
Patents, trademarks, copyrights pending
Future product research

(This section should describe, completely and concisely, the product, along with any proprietary features and future development plans.

If the product is highly technical, it must be toned down for easy comprehension. This is not the time for impressing or overwhelming potential investors with technical jargon.

In clear and uncomplicated words describe the product in detail indicating the nature and application, include material such as engineering studies, photographs, and selling brochures.

State how much R&D has been done, where it is in the development state, position on its life cycle, how long it will take to get it on the street, proprietary advantages: all in basic English so that lay investors can understand.

Discuss any patents, trade secrets, and other proprietary features.

Describe the characteristics which make it head and shoulders above anything else in the marketplace.

The Product section should be shorter than the Marketing section to reinforce the entrepreneur's awareness of the importance of the market.

Infatuation with the product rather than a cognizance of the market demand is a giant step backward towards rejection.

Some say that Steve Jobs at Apple was product-biased. As Apple began its backward slide, a marketer was brought in. The strategic move was a quick 180 degree reversal from product to market and Apple was on its way back up.)

VII. MARKET (value 20–30%)

Market definition, size, industry trends, and potential
Target market niche and growth parameters
Customer profile, demand, and a geographic analysis
Product differentiation and competitive advantage
Sales plan
Penetration strategy and distribution channels
Competition and response
Pricing
Maintaining a competitive edge

Marketing often gets short shrift at the hands of many would-be entrepreneurs. But venture capitalists rate a carefully devised marketing strategy as a critical component of a Business Plan.

It is essential to paint a clear picture of the market; its behavior, buying patterns, changes, beliefs, and attitudes to convince potential investors that the target market is well understood and sales targets are achievable.

There has to be an unserved market segment on which the entrepreneur can draw a bead. Remember:

> The best product will not sell unless there is a demand.

To describe an untapped market niche takes careful study, deliberate consideration, and a clear understanding.

There should be a description of the benefits to the customer to support the presumption of demand.

Investors want to know there is a definable customer base and gain confidence that the entrepreneur can do the job. Any objective analyses that confirm the market description, whether they are gathered from periodicals, sampling the population, Department of Commerce figures, market expert surveys, or whatever: should be included.

Startups often go awry because the entrepreneur went off half cocked: did not identify the market accurately or misread market demand or developed a magnificent off-target product or ignored competition or goofed in measuring market behavior.

Show a cognizance of competition and the expected competitive response. Name and discuss all major competitors, nature of competition: cut-throat or permissive, poorly-or well-financed.

Compare on the basis of price, share, performance, service, warranties, and other features. The strengths and weaknesses of competition must be evaluated. Finally, what is the competition likely to do to react.

Investors are motivated by growth potential above 20% and markets of $100 million or more. Narrow, unexpandable market crevices are less attractive.

Execution, or the ability to sell a product successfully, is even more important than the market identity itself or the product. That is why the nuts and bolts execution must be discussed.

Hyman Shwiel, Ernst & Whinney, said, "I know plenty of good ideas, I just don't know that many great people who can execute them."

VIII. MANAGEMENT (value 60%)

Organizational structure and organizational chart
Key managers including detailed resumes and references
Innovative ability
Profit consciousness and reputation
Compensation and incentives
Future Management Plans

(Management is the Jarvik-7 of all enterprises, bar none. This section of the Business Plan will include the key management team and include detailed resumes with highlights of their careers.

The experience, talent, and integrity of the management team are of primary concern to investors. Venture capitalists will conduct a thorough reference check of each member of the team.

Describe the key management team members, tell what the key roles will be, who will fill each position, and how each individual's talents will complement each other.

Detail the duties and responsibilities of each individual, career highlights, ownership share, and compensation.

The investors must be convinced that the management team is well qualified and talented in the field in which the company will serve. Investors put money in management more than products, more than markets, more than ephemeral expectations.

Arthur Rock is one of the country's most sophisticated investors. He was asked how he could fund such a variety of high tech firms when he did not have a highly technical background. He replied that he invested in people, not products.

Tommy Davis, the Mayfield Fund patriarch, provided a Business Plan outline for emerging entrepreneurs. The management team section was at the top.

Encore went public and did well, without a clearly-defined product but with a strong and prestigious management team. It was management which carried Encore through the public offering successfully.

If professional advisors are to be used, they can contribute to credibility. It is important to describe consultants, legal, accounting, public relations, advertising, bank, and other service organizations selected.)

IX. OPERATIONS

Location
Plant and equipment requirements
Manufacturing processes
Available capacity
Labor
Working capital needs
Geographic location strategy

This section will include how the product will be manufactured, including location, plant and equipment, capacity, labor, and manufacturing processes.

The location of the business should be discussed with the advantages and disadvantages of the site considering wage rates, unions, labor availability, proximity to markets, transportation, pertinent State, City, and Federal and related laws, and utilities.

The facilities in use or to be acquired should be discussed, leased or bought. Comments should be made on future plant and equipment needs, based on sales forecasts, including the cost of additional capacity and timing.

The manufacturing processes related to the business should be described including method of manufacture, control of quality, production, and inventory. Raw materials or components (including cost, source, and contracts) plus organization and purchasing; a breakdown of the fixed manufacturing costs should be detailed. There should also be a breakdown of variable costs of the product.

If the product is a mindset and not an actuality, some important R&D points should be covered:

The invention and a general description
Competitive advantage
The cost of development and beta testing
The time required to get a prototype developed
How it will be manufactured
Manufacturing advantages
Growth potential

Investors prefer to put their money into a known product rather than into R&D seed projects.

They are particularly chary about unknown R&D time and material costs, so similar projects should be coupled, if they exist.

Engineering costs in support of the prototype and subsequent manufacturing must be clarified. They are necessary and influence the pricing and market penetration. The Operations issues are:

Make or buy decision
Ease of manufacturing
Product unit cost
Level of quality and control
Cost control

Manufacturing plans are usually straightforward. Investors want to know what it takes in time, materials, and labor to manufacture a product.

The success of a startup revolves around the people in the front lines and entrepreneurs must show an awareness of people.

People are a company's most valuable asset.

People are crucial as backups to the lead in a musical. Without them a Harold Hill would likely stumble, singing "Seventy Six Trombones;" a Dolly Levi would be less than sensational singing "Hello Dolly" without vocal support; Johnny Jones would have a hard time of it singing "I'm a Yankee Doodle Dandy" without the people of the chorus providing a vocal backdrop and ongoing support.

To the extent that management is effective and successful in selecting, enticing, luring, hiring, training, motivating, and keeping employees, a startup can be made or broken.

Employee issues to be covered are:

Profile. What type of people will be working?
Employment. Lifetime? Unions? Training?
Compensation. Salaries. Stock Options. Profit Sharing. Bonuses and commissions. Other Benefits.
Culture. How does management think about people and their participation?

The most popular style is a bottom up, highly interactive group of employees, to ensure optimization of effort. Investors look more favorably on consensus management with quality control groups and employee participation and open door policies than the autocratic pedestal management.

"The key," says Bob Collings of Data Terminal Systems, one of the new breed of entrepreneurs, "is to discard the Mushroom Theory of Management. This theory advocates keeping employees in the dark and throwing a lot of manure on them. If you're going to manage a growing company, you have to concentrate on managing people, not ignoring them."

Briefly, a corporate culture which emphasizes employees participation and nurturing, should be expressed for they are the pivotal part of any company.)

X. GOALS AND OBJECTIVES

Short term goals
Long term objectives

Corporate culture
Manufacturing strategy
Market share expectations
Penetration level
Anticipated Market response
Revenue forecast
Profitability

(The goals and objectives should be directed toward an orderly growth, profitability, and a well positioned company. This is not an over the rainbow view. Waxing too poetic can be a disaster. This is the time for laudatory long term visions.)

XI. FINANCIAL (value 5–10%)

Three to five year pro forma forecasts
Income statements
Cash flow analyses
Balance sheets
Statements of changes in financial position
Cost/volume/profit analysis where appropriate
Proposed financing and capital structure

(Though a detailed financial forecast should appear in an appendix, there should also be about one page of information which includes a financial summary of the company: income statement, cash flow analysis, and balance sheet.

This is a reduced version of the finances of the company and should be easy to read. This information should address the problem of investment and permit the investor to make a judgment as to the potential future value of the investment made.

In the appendix should be financial forecasts to extend five years from the date of the investment. This is an arbitrary number of years within which businesses are expected to reach profitability.

Typically, all forecasts except the balance sheet show a monthly progression over the first two years and a quarterly progression for the remaining three years. There is most often a large loss in the initial startup phase, with reduction of losses until a breakeven at about two-three years.

The specific financial forecasts that are incorporate in a Business Plan are:

The Income Statement (Profit and Loss). Some operational footnotes should be included on the Income Statement to explain how certain totals were reached. Also, any deviations from industry norms should be explained.

The Cash Flow Forecast. This forecast is extremely useful to management in anticipating failures, problems, or successes. It should be updated monthly to help management in decision-making.

The Balance Sheet. The pro forma Balance Sheet helps investors evaluate the entrepeneur's awareness of asset management. The approach should conform with standard accounting practices so that the Balance Sheets are readable and reasonable.

Break Even Analysis. This consists of a chart, usually linear, displaying total costs vs. total revenues, over a time period: months or years. Break-even is reached when total revenues equal total costs. This point is valuable to both management and investors, since it permits assessment of financing needs.

The Financials must speak for themselves. They should not require interpretation and must not raise questions external to the business. Explanations should be limited to simple footnotes.

Under the proposed financing and capital structure section of the Business Plan, state how much money is needed, why it is needed, and what will be done with it. When negotiating money amounts, allow room for variations, and keep in mind future rounds of financing which will be needed.

If the company is already in operation, the capital structure should be explained and what effect funding will have on the source and use of funds.

If it is a startup, what funding has been received, how it has been spent, who the shareholders are, what their positions are in the firm, how much stock they own, and how much they paid for it.

An explanation of how the funds will be spent must be consistent with the financial forecasts.

If it is seed capital, a statement as to the development of the product and how the prototype development organization will be set up should be made.

It is mandatory to explain categorically how much of the money will be used for product development, R&D, marketing, manufacturing, capital equipment, etc.

It is critical to:

- Establish the need for funds in the amount requested and supported by the financial analysis and forecast.
- Demonstrate the ability to achieve investment goals or to repay indebtedness.
- Indicate an understanding of the financial implications of the business growth necessities.
- Show a realistic measurement of the planned business activity. That is, integrate the Business Plan with the Financial Plan.
- Do not include what is expected in percentages of ownership. Each case is different and negotiations must take place to accomplish an understanding.

XII. APPENDICES

Management structure (charts, additional resumes, etc.)
Historical financial information and support
Major assumptions
Append catalogue sheets, photographs, technical information, and brochures describing product/service
Letters of recommendation or endorsement
Pending lawsuits for or against

(The Appendices provides the reader with easy access to detailed information that supports the dialogue in the Business Plan.

It is important for the reader to get a broad view of the project without being mired in too much detail.

The entrepreneur makes tacit statements and those are backed up by the extraneous evidence in the Appendices.

Business Plans can be intimidating, and readers are apt to inactively read plans which are not in bite-sized pieces. The Appendices provides reinforcement for those who like to skim, speed read, or need supporting information.)

XIII. SUMMARY

The industry, the company, and its personnel
The opportunity

Timing
Product/market fit
Return on investment estimates
Risks involved

There is no cookie cutter approach to a Business Plan because each venture is unique, with its own product, market, management, style, and financial constraints.

A superstar cast with a proprietary product and a gaping market will get a VC nod of assent even if the Business Plan is scrawled on a paper table mat. But that is not the way it should be done.

Entrepreneur Rob Reis, Savi Technology, points out that the Business Plan must be a credible story with internal consistencies. Each part of the plan supports and confirms the other part. It should have clarity and openness.

The Business Plan should contain an element of excitement. Every Business Plan should come close to winning a blue ribbon at the Optimists' Convention. It is not an historical document or a commercial for the founders.

It must be of the right stuff; computer-generated scenarios in Business Plans are not impressive. Such electronic theatrics accomplish little and needlessly padding is anathema to a good plan.

Do not send out a plan without following a standard agenda or the plan will strike out.

One venture capitalist confessed, "We are so inundated with Business Plans that we look for something in the plan that will allow us to say no."

Reis suggests that any negative observations are better transmitted to potential investors verbally rather than in print.

Do be tongue tied. If you do not get funded, it may be because of an overuse of assumptions and adjectives.

The Director of the Center of Entrepreneurial Studies at NYU analyzed 80 Business Plans. Professor McMillan found that 55 plans were funded and 27 plans were not. Plans using more than 1.5 adjectives per noun or less than .25 per noun did not get funding. It is a lesson worth noting—not too many and not too few.

Be selective about sending out the Business Plan. Make sure the intended reader has the capacity to fund and the interest in the field. One of the quickest ways to get a rejection is to send it to a venture capitalist who does not fund that kind of business.

The Business Plan must address the following issues:

Strategy. How the goods or services are to be sold. Quantify and qualify the market, how large it is, what drives it, why customers will buy, and how it is segmented.

Customers. Give an estimated number, spendable income, behavior, motivation, and all of the factors that separate money from a buyer. The customer must be accurately described.

Sales. The Plan must detail how the product will be distributed and sold: by Reps, Distributors, In-house salespersons, Direct Mail, Executive Selling, or Franchising. The intended market techniques to be used must be told, that is, how it is planned to identify, contact, and sell to customers. Discuss the planned sales force and selling strategies for the various accounts, demographic areas, and geographic markets. The sales plan will determine how much money will be needed and what the costs of sales, administrative and general, as well as other, will be.

Competition. No Business Plan is credible unless it includes a realistic appraisal of the firm's competitors. The marketing section should include a calculated description of competition. The firms who will be the primary competitors should be measured with respect to strengths, weaknesses, and probable response. A concise and honest description of competition will add credibility. It will assure prospective investors that competition is out there and the entrepreneur is forearmed.

Advertising and Promotion. Comments should show how the market is going to learn about the product. There have been cases of successful startups which have had fully articulated advertising campaigns which have been inordinately successful. Remember, not all startups have been weaned on advertising. In Hyannis, Massachusetts, a small potato chip company pushed its brand name sales to record heights by word-of-mouth advertising! The total advertising budget was zero!

Southwest Airlines donated half a dozen free trips to winners of a Southern California food chain. The promotion provided Southwest with thousands of dollars of free advertising. A thirty second radio commercial would have cost more than $25,000! The six free trips were empty seats! In the matter of advertising and promotion, it is whatever fits.

Positioning. How the product is positioned in the market is a difficult, strategic choice which is the weighing and balancing of objectives, cost, pricing, demand, quality, service, and technology.

GETTING THE BUSINESS PLAN INTO GOOD HANDS

Venture Capitalists (VCs) get more Business Plans than they can analyze, often several a day, over the transom. They are Dead On Arrival (DOA). They are swept in like a tide and out in the same way. VC firms simply do not have the manpower to evaluate unsolicited plans. Reid Dennis, Institutional Venture Partners (IVP), said at a recent venture seminar, a Business Plan must be recommended by a friend or business acquaintance. By the way, Dennis reckoned that his firm funds about 2% of the Business Plans read. Don Valentine estimates that he has received three Business Plans every day for the past 15 years, about 15,000 plans. He has never gone through a Business Plan which was not recommended by a friend or business acquaintance. He funds less than 2% of the plans he reads. Dr. Bob Carlson, President of the Woodside Fund, estimates that 1–2% participation is their funding range. The typical pattern for the investigation scenario of 100 proposals presented to a venture capital firm or an SBIC might be:

50 discarded in five minutes or less
30 eliminated in a few hours or less
10 trashed after a close analysis of a week
5–8 gone after a detailed study of several weeks
2–5 accepted after a lengthy study of about a month
1–2 funded after all of the roadblocks are eliminated

SOME COMMON MYTHS

1. Use a professional writer. The Business Plan is a very personal document and its preparation must not be let to someone else. The entrepreneur must know the plan thoroughly, live, and breathe it. This understanding comes from involvement. It is an extension of the entrepreneur. A professionally prepared Business Plan is a turnoff as the entrepreneur is not the guiding force behind it.

2. The way it is packaged does not make any difference. It has been said that some venture capitalists are so conditioned that they think of Business Plans in terms of thickness! Do not believe it! A Business Plan should be no more than one-quarter to one-half an inch thick. It should be on bond paper, 8 by 11 inches is standard in commerce. The pages should be numbered. Use white space liberally. Provide ample borders on the sides, top, and bottom of the pages. Investors expect a Business Paln to be neatly typed with a standard, businesslike type font, purged of poor grammar, and spelling errors. The diagrams should be professional (at least not scratchings). Bind the plan in a simple but secure cover, loosely bound with a clear plastic dime store cover will do nicely. A plan which is too polished, too slick, and terribly chic, can raise the eyebrows of venture capitalists. Trendy disco plans will be trashed as quickly as an entrepreneur appearing in sneakers, jeans, and a large peace sign on a dirty tee shirt. Consider the statistics from one Boston venture capital firm. Of 1200 business proposals received during a period of several months, 600 were read, 45 were researched, and 14 funded. They discarded, without reading, Business Plans which did not have a reasonable format, were not easy to read, or were hard to follow. George Crandell, Brentwood Associates, remembers two cardboard boxes containing 12 volumes of looseleaf Business Plans. "We knew we weren't going to read them."

3. Get ONE investor. It is an inescapable shoo-in that there will be many investors and investor groups, rarely one. It is only important that the entrepreneur and the investors get along at the onset. If there is a lurking doubt, the result may be friction downstream.

4. Describe how the product works. Do not! There are two reasons. In the early stages, the technology changes rapidly and, no matter what level of distribution defined, the plans will go beyond the entrepreneur's control.

5. Business Plans should be heavy in detail. Only include detail which is in the mainstream of evaluating an investment decision. Cumbersome detailed strategic data dilutes the quality of the Business Plan.

6. Discuss the DEAL in the Business Plan. The DEAL is too diverse. There are so many variables. It is better left for verbal negotiations with serious investors.

7. Lay all risks out on the table. Risk is very much a personal perception. It is an excellent subject to leave for investor discussion. While valuable

and appropriate, it is better suited for eyeball to eyeball discussion than laid out in the Business Plan.

8. Be deliberately conservative. Be accurate or even optimistic. A conservative Business Plan will not sell an investor, sorry. Investors typically discount the blue sky forecasts by 50% anyway, some even higher! Try to be as accurate as possible and consider what can be achieved as a believer. No exaggerations, however.

9. Track record is not important. It can be important! The Plan should include where all of the management team worked and how well they performed in the past in any business. Without a doubt, this is a significant issue when assessing management's ability.

10. Send a miniplan to investors first. Experience has shown that this does not work. It is much better to have the entire Business Plan available to each and every potential investor.

11. Hand deliver the Business Plan to investors. Only if the entrepreneur is well established will this work. A third-party referral is far better with a followup mailing or third-party delivery. Do not pass them out like calling cards!

Entrepreneurs bomb when they assault the VC Center on Sand Hill Road in Menlo Park and hand out Business Plans like bagels.

12. Save it all for the Business Plan. If preselling can be done through a friend or a third party, it will set the stage for the Business Plan. If someone is well respected and has good liaison with an investor group—consultant, banker, lawyer, accountant, or another entrepreneur—let them prep the investors with a precursor of the new venture. This is another way of getting the Business Plan read.

13. The business will grow in a straight line. Venture capitalists would rather see entrepreneurs adjust their planning to allow for funding at various stages of the company's growth. The line is wavy, always.

SOME UNCOMMON TRUTHS ABOUT A BUSINESS PLAN

1. It is the price of a ticket for admission to the investment process.
2. It is the pivotal first and maybe only shot.
3. The company name is important.

4. Geographic location is important.
5. Length is pivotal.
6. Quality of the Business Plan cover is important.
7. Arrange it appropriately with a Table of Contents chapters in sequential order.
8. The Executive Summary is a miniplan, the carrot.
9. The Business Plan must explain in quantitative and qualitative terms the benefits to the consumer of the firm's product or service.
10. It must present hard evidence of the marketability of the product or service.
11. Writers tend to understate the competition.
12. It must justify the sales strategy chosen.
13. The Business Plan must explain and verify the level of product development which has been reached and describe in detail the manufacturing process as well as the related costs.
14. It must portray the founders as a team of experienced, motivated, and congenial managers with complementary business skills.
15. A lack of experience in a specific field is deadly.
16. It must transmit as high an overall rating as possible of the new venture's product development and team sophistication.
17. A mediocre idea with a well experienced team is far better than a great idea with an inexperienced team.
18. It must contain believable financial forecasts, with key data explained and documented.
19. Some Business Plans suffer from Lotus-itis, the profusion of spreadsheet information.
20. It must be easily and concisely explainable in a well-orchestrated oral presentation.
21. A well written Business Plan will tell what the entrepreneur, founders, and the new venture expect to accomplish 3–5 years down the road.
22. It must show clearly how investors can cash out in 3–5 years, with appropriate capital appreciation.
23. Targeting only the most potentially receptive investor groups will avoid wasting valuable time as startup funds erode rapidly.

A Venture Capitalist's opinion of what should come through in a Business Plan:

1. INTEGRITY. This is basic, but often overlooked or assumed. It implies more than honesty. It includes a willingness to take responsibility,

authority, and accountability. It also presumes that the entrepreneur will admit mistakes, face facts, and not let ego prevail over all.

2. MOTIVATION. This is the key issue. Does the entrepreneur want to build the largest and best firm than can possibly be developed without reckless haste or foolish risk? Or does the entrepreneur want a nice, comfortable company that moves slowly and safely along? Perhaps the entrepreneur wants prestige from esoteric developments that do not have volume sales as a goal. Are the founders looking for perks; company cars, spacious offices, salaries, expense account, and golden parachutes? What is their underlying motivation?

3. MARKET NICHE. The entrepreneur who has a handle on the market segment is the one most likely to make it. Interest is only in what people want to buy, have both the capacity and willingness to buy, soon and in large quantities. Though the entrepreneur uses statistical data and other analytical tools, he gets right up nose-to-nose with customers so that they are understood.

4. EXPERIENCE AND SKILLS. The entrepreneur starting a firm should have some experience in the field or have shown some capabilities. The entrepreneur should have managed similar operations of comparable size.

Investors do not want managers to learn at their expense. Entrepreneurs should have the technical capability to create in the selected field. Though removed from the lab, it may be necessary to judge creative work and stimulate research.

5. FINANCIAL SKILLS. An entrepreneur should be able to do more than balance a checkbook. It is not necessary to be a CPA or to be an accountant. But without understanding cost information and financial basics, it will be difficult to make cost/benefit analyses, set prices, allocate costs for R&D, estimate market penetration budgets, and understand resource management.

6. LEADERSHIP. This defies description, for the entrepreneur must be a leader. To inspire, make hard decisions, good choices, motivate, and maintain respect; all are part of it. The entrepreneur makes things happen.

7. PRODUCT vs SERVICE. Product startups are preferred because the design can be sold repetitively. They are iterative and not one-shot. The more sold, the more profits that can be generated. With experience, costs

can be reduced, modification made, and further profits realized. On the other side, manufactured products typically cost more for design, beta-testing, and reaching markets.

8. HIGH-TECH PRODUCTS. High-tech products reach markets after extensive R&D. They are more difficult to copy. It is easier to strike higher prices and profit margins. Competition is less intense. More measureable technical advantage is necessary and can be calculated. It is a simpler task to appraise the competence of the team in a sophisticated area, in terms of hiring. Experience in high technology tends to be more precise than in low-tech or middle-tech or services.

9. MARKETS. Market size should be above $100 million per year and growing more than 20% annually. However, venture funding is becoming so competitive, lesser markets are now being accepted.

10. COMPETITION. A large market share in a small market is preferred to a small share in a large market. It is undesirable to take on companies with huge resources. Smaller markets allow a low profile entry, not threatening to large competitors. A market position can be firmly established. Head to Head with Big Blue is almost assuredly a death knell if an entrepreneur wants to do it.

11. THE COMPANY. Who are you? A Business Plan must show clearly and precisely the nature of the new venture and its market, the amount of money needed, sales and earnings forecasts, and the makeup of the management team. Like a resume, the Business Plan's purpose in life is to get an interview for its writer.

12. READABILITY. The first minute of reading is the key to a Business Plan. It is the equivalent of first eye contact in romancing.

13. BREVITY. There are some things that venture capitalists uniformly want in a Business Plan. One is BREVITY. Some venture capitalists argue that 12 pages should be the maximum while no one wants to look at anything greater than 40 pages.

7

HOW TO RAISE MONEY

ESTABLISHING CAPITAL REQUIREMENTS

Raising money involves three issues:

- AMOUNT,
- SOURCE, and
- the DEAL

Amount

The buck starts here. No investor can be contacted without having the barrel loaded:

1. Exactly what AMOUNT will be needed?
2. How will it be spent?
3. What will the investor get in return?

It is important to know three AMOUNTS:

Minimum—without which it is not a go;

Desired—which is a tradeoff of ownership and comfort;
Maximum—which may or may not be acceptable because of concomitant tradeoffs.

A danger of being chintzy and opting for a *minimum* AMOUNT, smaller than absolutely needed is that a funding shortfall can hamstring a startup. Trying to save the AMOUNT of money asked for will have practically no effect on the investment decision. Ten percent more or less startup money will have only a smidgin of impact on a yea or nay from the investor decision-maker. This pinpoints the necessity of knowing precisely how many dollars will be needed. The dollars necessary for each milestone must be calculated to arrive at the total AMOUNT. Also estimate the timeframes. The *desired* AMOUNT will have to be supported with the investors. The *maximum* AMOUNT will be difficult to get, and the ownership tradeoff may be more than an entrepreneur will want to give up. Also, funding may be refused because the dollars are too many, even though it is a gangbuster project. The farther up the development step ladder the project reaches before canvassing for money, the less is the uncertainty. For the investors, risk is proportionately reduced. Therefore, less money will be needed and smaller hunks of ownership will be chewed up. There is a valid argument for getting the total AMOUNT for the project, up front. A contention holds that, with long term funding in place, the entrepreneur can devote all efforts to getting the new venture up to speed instead of chasing money. The difficulty of raising money has a direct relationship to the AMOUNT. The greater the AMOUNT the more difficult will be the task. The AMOUNT must also be realistic and related to the size of the project. If the startup is a small business, it is a waste of time to ask for $3 million or more. There are no blue-sky dollars raining out of the heavens. Getting money has always been a tradeoff for a piece of the action. The number of dollars sought must be weighed against the size of the project, how much ownership is to be horsetraded, and the risks/benefits for investors. The name of the money gathering game has dollars signs vs ownership, percentages vs ROI all over it. It is a simplistic application of the Zero Sum theory which behavioral scientists developed forty years ago.

Applied to the new ventures, this theory suggests that a zero sum equilibrium is maintained. No money from investors permits 100% ownership. If money is invested on one side, the entrepreneur must surrender a compensating share of ownership on the other side of the ledger to maintain the equilibrium.

The AMOUNT is derived from the following three steps:

1. SEED. An idea whose time has come.

- Pre-venture or Germination
- Research and Development
- Facilities acquisition
- Forming an organization
- Beta-test*
- One to two years
- $50,000–$200,000

How long will it take? (Time is money.) This is the piggy bank equity necessary to start from point zero. The money required may not need to reach deep pockets for starters. It is the bare bones step. It takes few dollars, but some hard cash is required for a telephone deposit, postage stamps, letterhead stationery, a computer, and utilities. Help can come from friends or relatives in some dollars or sweat equity (work for no pay, shares). It is usually birthed in the living room, on a card table or in a den. When the living room or den is overcrowded, the next move is down to the basement or garage, with borrowed or cast off furniture. Then there will be R&D, beta-testing, shop equipment, and a shoe box with a few dollars. Sandra Kurtzig had two shoe boxes; one for incoming dollars and another for outgoing dollars. The seed stage is very small time.

Though seed money is the first step, the entrepreneur should consider subsequent financing. Seed investment is not a guarantee of next call for funding. The question to ask is, "Will any of the investors be available for additional money?"

2. STARTUP. This piggy went to market.

- Ad-venture or First Round
- Prototype developed
- Manufacturing established
- Recruitment of key personnel
- Marketing strategy established
- Product introduced to market
- Competitive response

---

*Alpha testing a product is in house-beta testing a product out of the house.

- One year to eighteen months
- $200,000–$1,000,000

In the first round financing, the founder, family, and friends drop out, for the dollars begin to take on large numbers. Others often not involved in first round will be certain professional investors, R&D partnerships, and seed venture capitalists. They will be replaced with professional individual investors and venture capitalists. If a venture capitalist firm participates, they often spread the investment, becoming the lead investor for a small interest and invite other venture capital firms to participate. This has the advantage of reducing the risk, making the second round easier, and provides the new venture with a valuable ally.

STARTUP money is needed to underwrite launching the new venture. The product is introduced to the market, encounters market behavior, feedback is evaluated, and a response is made. Typically, it is negative cash flow time as a market position is formulated. Fine tuning makes necessary changes in the product or market strategy.

3. RAPID GROWTH. Market explosion takes place.

- Mezzanine or Second Round
- Rapid expansion takes place
- Labor force triples or quadruples
- Infusion of additional capital necessary
- Negative cash flow continues
- One to two years
- $500,000–$4,000,000

This is the time of rapid expansion in production, personnel, equipment, and negative cash flow. As sales take off, the core organization expands correspondingly, from a marble to a bowling ball. The scenario is a chaotic ballooning of the company; equipment, personnel, and activities increase geometrically. It is not unusual to have the basic startup firm expand by a factor of five or more in the first six months of RAPID GROWTH. Cash flow and debt financing will not accommodate the growth. Additional funding will be required, for the RAPID GROWTH alligator must be fed. How long will it take to turn the corner and become profitable? How much money will be needed to carry the negative cash flow? The investors will want to know. That is the rub, someone said. Quirky as it might seem, estimates must be made. Professor Fran Jabara, founder and director of the Center for Entrepreneurship at Wichita State University in Kansas sums it up accurately, "Managing growth is one of the greatest challenges in startups."

> The three steps add up to the total AMOUNT needed for three to five years. Full funding—$1,000,000 to $5,000,000

The reality is that most startups start with short term, incremental funding; a mincing step at a time, and it is ever a Catch-22 situation as to money and ownership. Because most entrepreneurs are so enthusiastic about the project, they are often willing to give away the store, to rue the folly later. There are two good reasons for incremental funding; it is easier to obtain and less ownership has to be given away. The bad news is that should any milestone goals be missed, there is the risk of not being able to get back to the funding trough for additional money. This, even though a milestone might not be reached through no fault and though it might not affect the ultimate profitability goals except in time. Once the product is developed, it is easier to get the next round. If the product is on the market, it is still easier to get a third round of money. As each of these steps is passed, not as much has to be given away. We are not required to give up as much as if we had asked for funding for all three steps, in advance. Long term funding provides a security blanket for the entrepreneur but increases the investor's exposure. Demanding full funding will require giving up more than 50% of the company, that is for sure. Because a five-year equity funding is a larger amount than short-term, incremental money: it is more difficult to obtain. All the above are guesstimates and must be made, if only suppose. It is up to the entrepreneur to carefully calculate the dollars needed (ignore cents), how and when the money will be spent, with backup facts and believable explanations. Potential investors know that these are "off the wall" assumptions. They will be influenced by how skillfully and convincingly the assumptions are presented. That is the way to turn on the green light. Investors buy people, not pro formas, and not boilerplate enthusiasm. After each meeting with potential investors, a critique is a must. The feedback should be evaluated, the questions asked, and the "way we were" should be used to hone the AMOUNT. Day by day the presentation will become more effective, and the money sought will make more sense.

Alternatively, if the equity is not a capital investment but a loan, the project may be strapped with heavy monthly payments, every month. The payback schedule will include interest payments of about 2% above the prime rate. Such loans are usually unsecured and payable over 3–5 year period.

It is also highly unlikely that a loan will be granted without a tradeoff for some share of ownership, though smaller than for a capital investment. Stock warrant sweeteners may be included.

The AMOUNT will be impacted by whether it is invested money or borrowed money. The comfort level of these two issues must be determined.

What this all means is that it is critical to know exactly how much money is needed. The amount is a critical issue with many ramifications, but do not leave home without it.

SOURCES

Real Dollars

Personal Investment.   At the outset, the most common method for financing is for the entrepreneur to use personal assets. Savings accounts and stocks are liquid and useable. A second mortgage on a home is a common method or refinancing the first mortgage. Refinance the car, vacation home, or any asset which has equity.

Family, Friends, and Friendly Investors.   Good sources for entrepreneurs rich in ideas but poor in wherewithal are family and friends. Outside investors are often willing to take a flier for a few thousand. They are given stock for pennies which can redeemed for dollars later. It is rolling dice for them, a Las Vagas crapshoot. Individual investment targets are about 40% return on investment on an annual basis, 5 times investment in 5 years, and 30 times investment return in 10 years.

Venture Capitalists.   The equity needs over the next few years indicates a requirement in excess of $6 billion. Neil Brownstein, a venture capitalist of Menlo Park, California, estimates that industry does not have enough money to sponsor half the required amount. What this foretells is that money may not get easier to obtain. Once a startup is committed, seed money is necessary. There is a coterie of Seed Venture Capitalists. In the last five years, about 3000 startups were funded by the venture capital industry. In the range of 10% were seed-level fundings. Venture capitalists look for about a 25% annual return on investment. In the early 1980's, higher rates were obtainable, but those salad days are gone. Their portfolios opt for at least 3 times investment return in five years and about 10 times investment return in 10 years.

They want a market size of about $100 million to $250 million, a market share target of about 20%, and revenue goals not less than $50-million annually.

The product/service should be able to reach a public offering in less than 5 years.

Corporate equity partners.   Corporations can often fit new products into their line or are looking for outside opportunities for diversification. Cash cows are prime prospects, more often so if the startup is compatible with their product family.

Joint venturing.   Participating with another group is an option. Sometimes a company will act as a joint venture partner. They might have excess plant time or idle machine time but do not have the manpower or resources to develop the new product. A joint venture may provide financial or management support for a slice of the pie. It may be that there is a group in the midst of the same project or one that is compatible. It might be a viable decision to plunge ahead in lockstep with someone else and pool resources.

Banking Institutions.   A survey conducted by *Entrepreneur Magazine* studied the question of relations between bankers and entrepreneurs. It found that bankers are more comfortable in dealing with big business and not so comfortable with small businesses which characterize start-ups. What image springs to mind when a banker is mentioned? The jokes abound. Bankers will loan money to anyone who can prove that they do not need it. A banker is a person who lend an umbrella on a sunny day. A banker is a person who wanted to be an accountant but lacked the joyful personality. Ken Libkin, Imperial Bank regional VP, said, "When you say 'entrepreneur,' that implies to me that the individual is just in a start-up mode. In that case, he may in fact be expecting from a commercial banker a function that is more appropriately assigned to a venture capitalist. A banker is a lender with the expectation of being repaid. Banks do not intentionally make investments in that (start-up) business." They cannot tolerate the risk of loans based on an investment theology of hopes and dreams. Commercial banks, Mortgage banks, and Savings and Loans are in the business of lending money with great safety and not investing in chancy startups. That does not make them loan averse to entrepreneurs. Their preference is more experiential, initial and round and beyond. Milt Koult, maverick entrepreneur and founder of Horizon Air in the Northwest, has found, "Bankers are delighted to deal with entrepreneurs who are beyond the start-up phase." Banking institutions are stogy and asset-based. But they do have the gold and make startup loans under certain conditions. They check references carefully. The friendly bankers want to know the entrepreneur. They prefer to help entrepreneurs who have money in the project or have some asset at risk. Also, banks relish OPM (Other People's Money) in a project.

The conventional banking wisdom bases loans on the five C's of credit:
Character
  Capacity
    Capital
      Conditions
        Collateral

Under most conditions, banks insist upon collateral to guarantee loans. Borrowing money requires collateral against which a loan can be secured. They will loan cash secured by the equity in a home, car, commercial property, stock, and savings. A good credit rating is a plus. They will want to know if the collateral has true liquidity. Should the lender be forced to foreclose, is the collateral easily convertible into cash so that the lender can recover the loan? Keep in mind that the friendly banker does not want to foreclose and will not make a loan for a bad startup with 19-carat gold collateral. Typically, local banks can be counted on for about 40–60% of the appraised value of an asset. By the way, a friend or a relative can provide collateral for a loan, or even cosign a note. European merchant banks have practiced participatory banking for years and make it work. Japanese and Hong Kong banks get such low yields at home that they are potential lenders. The new generation, creative U.S. bankers are beginning to see the light and are getting into some acts. They occasionally get into a venture on behalf of long-established customers, or for bank customers who have excess money and are looking for investment opportunities, risk opportunities, equity kickers, or loan packages.

Lenders of the last resort.   If the loan is too risky for banks or government agencies, an asset-based lender (ABL) may be willing to provide cash. ABLs lay claim to filling an important gap in capital structure by extending credit in the face of pro formas that horrify standard lenders. They may accept as collateral tangible assets that would give the shivers to even banks' own ABL groups.

Once castigated as a gang of break-nosed buzzards, ABLs use unusual assets where conventional sources may not. Some ABLs exist. However, most of the independent ABL operations have been picked up by banks. Some banking institutions have started their own. An ABLs annualized target yield is in the high twenties! It will not be cheap! ABL loans come dearly. A four-to six-point fee is common (each point is one percent of the total loan). That does not include a litany of fixed and variable add-on charges for loan origination, packaging, collateral management, accounting, and closing costs. It will include penalties for late payments. The borrower will have to pay all collection and legal fees in the event of default. In addition, they might tack on monthly service charges.

They may be thought of as loan sharks but they are a creative and potential dollar source at the end of the road.

Though it is not the most desirable source for cash, it may be a port in the storm.

Government Agencies.   Business Development Corporation (BDC). This is a category of private or public investment company that, by law, must place 70% of its capital in venture equity investments. It must also provide "significant managerial assistance" to portfolio companies.

U.S. Small Business Administration (SBA). The SBA will guarantee up to 90% of a loan made by banks and other lenders up to a maximum of $500,000. The SBA will make direct loans of not more than $150,000 when a potential business+borrower has been rejected by two banks. The SBA currently provides seven services, including direct loans, guaranteed loans, management assistance, publications and audio visual aids, and advocacy.

Small Business Investment Company (SBIC). There are some SBICs that will invest or lend money. An SBIC is licensed by the SBA and frequently has private capital as well as money borrowed from the government available to finance small businesses.

Minority Enterprise Small Business Investment Companies (MESBIC). For persons of minority groups, there are special types of SBIC's known as MESBIC's, which loan exclusively to members of minority groups. The SBA has the list.

Public Venture Capital Partnerships (PVCP). The PVCPs offer investment units smaller than traditional venture capital funds and create a window for the affluent investor. The $60-million Merrill Lynch Limited Partnership pioneered the market in 1982 by offering units at $5,000 a share.

Small Business Innovation Research (SBIR). There must be less than 500 employees. The grants are $550,000. They do not have to be repaid.

State and City government funds. It is necessary to investigate and research all agencies for states and cities vary. When amounts needed are small ($250,000 or less), many new firms in the Northeast go to the Massachusetts Technology Development Corporation (MTDC). The state agency was formed in 1979 to convince bankers to make loans to new ventures.

There are other variations on the public fund theme. There is public money around; startup grants, funds for study, and for special projects. It is knowing where the money is hidden and how to get it, for there are tricks to the trade.

Jigsaw capital. This capital funding is fitted together in complex packages; leases, debt, partnerships, investor cash, vendor equity, credit lines, you name it. It is a flexible, adaptive strategy adjusted to the collateral form and availability. It is the bits and pieces, a Mickey Mouse approach; a little here and a little there.

Networking. "Money By Getting Around" is a useful alternative in scrambling for bucks. The character of entrepreneurship lends itself to networking, conversing with almost anybody who will listen.

The key to selectively communicating—with the right people.

The word gets around and friends tell friends. Before long there is a common body of words circulating among available investors and some projects get heated.

Networking is often used to get the project known. Not only talking among potential investors, venture capital partners but consultants, accountants, lawyers, and financial planners are finding startup linkages a viable strategy for portfolios.

(In networking, key elements are withheld to protect the concept from being stolen.)

In this seredipitous process, the ganglia are extended and one never knows which encounter will be meaningful.

Unreal Dollars

Non-money is commonly used to reduce hard dollars needed, as it can assume the properties of money without being green.

A rule of thumb for startups is that at least half of the money raised in startups comes from non-money sources. It is a ploy which knowledgeable entrepreneurs exploit.

Non-money alternatives have worked wonders for many new ventures.

Using Vendor's Resources is not a naughty expression.   Such shrewd exploitation of non-money resources will allow what would otherwise require hard-to-come-by cash.

Even though Steve Jobs has millions stashed for his new venture, NeXT, Inc., he used non-money sources to a fare-thee-well with great success. Vendors and non-money providers were happy with the deal for it gave them a potential Apple Computer opportunity to make a killing.

Barter is a viable alternative to cash.   Though the word "barter" conjures thoughts about trading marbles for bubblegum cards or a dozen Grade AA eggs and a pig for a few housecalls by the country MD, the same concept can work in a startup situation.

It might be possible to barter some of the research for a necessary addition to the startup. Barter shares of stock for rent, etc. Due bills can be bartered. (This is for services or products in trade for needed resources).

". . . most of the Fortune 500 companies are involved in barter at some level," says Dave Wallach, president of the American Trade Association.

A study by Stanford University forecases that 15% of all business in the U.S. will be conducted by barter by 1992.

Startups are so cash intensive, leasing instead of owning equipment is the only way to go.   Consider that no working or fixed asset has collateral value until at least 18 months have passed and a certain paydown has taken place. The collateral value is usually the paydown amount. This suggests that capital acquisitions (rather than leasing) are never the highest and best use of money in a cash intensive situation.

Furthermore, firms which elect to buy rather than lease, find their capital tied up in non-liquid assets. Any glich in the startup scenario is found unsupportable. It describes one of the major contributing factors which causes 80% of startups to close shop within two or three years.

Used, instead of new, is a good choice when it makes economic sense.   Acquiring used equipment is at a cheaper price than new. If the condition will permit weathering the first year or two maintenance-free, this is a satisfactory option. The monthly debt service is less. Fixed costs are the bane of the existence of a startup.

On the flip side, better deals may be stuck with new equipment where there is a larger margin with which to play.

Another consideration must be Operating Costs.   Under certain conditions, new equipment is the current state of the art instead of the past's best. It may offer some economies which will support a buy decision. New equipment can be faster, warrantied, maintenance free, and operate at a lower cost; so much so as to support monthly payments.

Not long ago a major airline was faced with a new/used decision. Used airliners were available for a fraction of the sticker price of new aircraft. However, the new generation machines had a total operating cost of $1000 an hour less than the older and cheaper, used aircraft. The airline flew 13 hours a day, six days a week. The new generation aircraft provided an operating cost savings of $312,000 per month, enough to cover the total monthly lease payments!

Non-money devices are intended to replace cash. It differentiates between buying, borrowing, begging, scheming, renting, leasing, delayed payments, and contracting. Non-money resources are in different forms, sources, amounts, security, values, and payback expectations. The participants vary in the way they quantify and qualify non-money options and needs. The exploitation of non-money resources is highly personal and intuitive and varied. One new venture, started in Silicon Valley, reached $10-million annual sales in seven years. The quartet started out at the kitchen table with only holes in their pockets. They used credit cards and

extended payment schedules, a poor man's float. Vendors were cooperative and deferred payment terms were eschewed with the promise of future
business. The four entrepreneurs proffered cheap warrants to buy stock to
some vendors in lieu of payment. Most vendors have a bit of the entrepreneurial spirit and are not risk averse. Moreover, vendors were gambling full retail dollars with wholesale green. The four founders later took
out bank loans on personal computers, VCRs, diamond rings, heirlooms,
furniture, cars and third mortgages on homes. Brown bagging lunches, the
foursome were their own handypersons. From cleaning lavoratories to
typing elegant letters to presidents of Fortune 500 companies, bootstrap-
ping was in the finest genre. They were so non-money oriented and such
workaholics that, when the four founders were replaced, the replacements
lamented that it took two to do the work of each founder at half the salary!
The two SOURCES of startup dollars are money and non-money. Both can
be exploited with success but must be treated differently.

Deal

How the DEAL is put together can spell disaster or success for the two
parties involved.

DEAL structure is the key.

Entrepreneurs should run deal expectations past friends, bankers, anyone to get a feel of if what they want and should have is realistic and
achievable.

The startup may be a second coming of Microsoft, but if a bad DEAL
is struck by the entrepreneur, it might well have been the Osborne Computer startup as far as what the entrepreneur gets for his blood, sweat, and
tears.

The DEAL is what made more than $350 million for Bill Gates at
Microsoft. There is no template for a DEAL. Each one is unique.

The time to get a DEAL fixed in cement is in the beginning. Verbal
understandings have a way of changing. Once the DEAL is cut, there is no
changing, no remembrance of "but you said." Paper every promise, each
understanding; if only in a note of intent.

Venture capital firms follow set formulas, and they are not out to cheat
the entrepreneur. Nevertheless, it is lawyer time, and the entrepreneur

should have a legal eagle in the aerie. Some entrepreneurs want to strike deals based on their special project, how much work they have done, what they know about the technology, what dedicated workers they are, and why this is a special investment. They have no idea of what the real world will accept. Venture capitalist Don Valentine suggests that the entrepreneur should be sure to state what is in it for the investor and make clear what the entrepreneur wants. That is a critical focus.

There are three types of negotiations in making a DEAL:

1. **Problem solving** to get the DEAL as a win-win. Both parties have common goals and little dissension exists. This is a comfortable situation, and both parties describe priorities and aggressively apply effort toward a solution in the interest of both, hand in hand. In problem solving, when a large problem cannot be solved, it can be broke into small solvable issues. What remains is often negotiable.

2. **Discussion.** Then the atmosphere is a little more cautious. Heavy negotiations and self interest dominate this style. Preparation, communications, understanding, and patience are extremely important.

3. **Battling.** This is the nitty gritty when both parties believe that they deserve more than the other side is willing to give. It may look like no deal at all. It is important to hang in there and not let go. Both sides may have to examine concessions, a partial DEAL, arbitration, or other options.

Terms and conditions are everything and are negotiable! One shrewd negotiator said, "I would buy anything for a dollar down and a dollar a week." The founder of the offshore drilling equipment company, SEDCO, started with one and then two more ancient drilling rigs held together with rusty bolts and bailing wire. The money? Almost nothing. But it got the entrepreneur into business.

An opportunity popped up when a competitor was left high and dry with five huge drilling rigs. The entrepreneur was able to strike a very favorable DEAL. The reason? Because SEDCO was up and running, a far cry from just a notion.

SEDCO was on its way to becoming one of the world's largest.

A pot-sweetening financial gimmick is the Equity Kicker. It is a ploy to get money by offering an option to buy future equity. Knowledgeable investors find the Equity Kicker option appealing. The Equity Kicker price for purchase options does not have to be the $.30 per share the founders paid nor would the price be the $10 public offering price. It can be at some attractive price in between. But it must be remembered that when the options are executed, it dilutes the value of outstanding shares. There is no free Hero sandwich.

There are certain smart steps which can be taken to increase the probability of a desired DEAL:

1. Know how much money is needed. Be able to defend the AMOUNT. Know how every dollar will be spent. Know the minimum required investment, the median, and the high end. Be flexible.
2. What will the investors get for their investment? It is important to look at the capital contribution and the Rate Of Return. There are hundreds of deals floating around. Why should an investor put money into this project?
3. Remember that the investors have the dollars. They ring the cash register.
4. Do not consider an AMOUNT for an investor which will not show at least 20–40% ROI annually over a four or five year period. It is not necessary to go above a 40% ROI.
5. Give deep thought to ownership. How much can be given away? Again, the low end, the median, and the highest giveaway.
6. Give consideration to taking on investors. Are they necessary? Can we be self funding? Do we want to stay self funded? Do we have a choice?
7. All DEALS must be in writing. When an agreement is concluded, even if it is over a cup of coffee, put it in writing.
8. Have mock negotiations. This should be a wide-open role modeling of what the investors might ask for and what they will settle on.
9. No formal agreement should be without legal counsel. It is worth the money and an absolute necessity.
10. Do not let a DEAL get away. Be realistic! There is no second time around.
11. In the ideal, unobtainable world the entrepreneur gets lots of money to ensure no financial crunch, is not loaded with a high debt repayment schedule, and does not give up one percent of ownership.

When raising money, entrepreneurs have knitted together complex DEALS using unusual vehicles:

1. When Encore Computer could not get money from one source, they would end up mixing a private placement by individual investors with debt and equity investment by two corporate partners.
2. When the going gets tough, the tough get going. "Ya gotta knock on doors" could be the corporate slogan for a San Francisco startup, the Megaphone Company. They mounted a do-it-yourself syndication of 25 limited partnership units and raised over $1 million for 29% of the company's equity. Then they decided on a syndicated equipment leasing package for special purpose hotline answering machines needed all over the country. This $1-million dollar lease line required them to give up only one-tenth as much of the Megaphone Company as an equivalent equity financing would have cost.
3. Partners are often a viable option. When Charles River Data Systems Inc., a 12-year-old firm, needed funds to develop a new 32-bit computer, they took on a partner, then another which was a potential customer, and a Japanese computer firm who saw the potential for the Orient. Later another firm put up funds and was a potential reseller of Charles River's new computer products as part of their own local network systems.
4. Occasionally, interest rates on conventional loans put the money out of the reach of entrepreneurs. Educational Insights tapped into one federal loan program not specifically aimed at new businesses. They were able to get a $2-million industrial revenue bond with 11% to finance construction for a new headquarters, warehouse, and assembly area. A comparable commercial loan would have been 14.5%. Industrial revenue bonds are a viable alternative.
5. Sara Addis launched a house-sitting business with no cash. She had just six elderly people who were willing to work for her at house-sitting. Today her nationally franchised corporation is expected to gross $7 million and is growing rapidly with operations planned in Canada and Japan for international starters. "I'm not saying it hasn't been tough. You sweat blood most of the time. But we've been so successful up to now and I foresee a fantastic future."
6. There is a state fund in Indiana that raises venture money from private businesses. It drew International CMOS Technology from

the Silicon Valley to the Midwest. The financing deal was for 40% of the company by a Korean firm which included a technology exchange pact.

7. When Myra Evans wanted to raise money for a gourmet Italian ice cream project, she took her former colleagues at Goldman Sachs a taster. Through a private placement she offered 49 shares of stock in Gelato at $5000 a share. Within 45 days, she raised almost a quarter of a million. Evans held onto 51% sweat equity. In the middle of the second $450,000 placement, Gelato Modo is offering 45 shares at $10,000 per share.

8. One computerized voicemail equipment startup could not get its first round funding. A potential customer put up financing in exchange for 28% of the firm's equity. Within a few months a private investment company guaranteed a bank loan in exchange for a 6% equity interest.

9. A housewife, Colleen King, started assembling computer circuit boards in her kitchen. "I had absolutely no knowledge of electronics when I started. I literally fell into the business." In eight years her business developed into $25 million annual sales with 430 employees and five plants. She recently sold out.

Entrepreneurs must manage time wisely in the pursuit of money and survive for double the time they had expected. They must learn the difference between just-looking and a qualified investor. The entrepreneur must be diligent and persistent. There will be numerous rebuffs; doors slammed, phone calls ignored, too-busy-call-in-a-few-months responses, sorry-funds-are-oversubscribed, not-our-field; disappointments one after another. Entrepreneurs must be able to get up, brush those off, and more forward with eternal hope in their hearts. Gathering enough money to get the project off the ground is a difficult but rewarding experience. It takes dedication and an unrelenting pursuit of every opportunity. Raising money is a many-faceted undertaking. If a startup is wildly successful, it is often believed by the entrepreneur that too much was given away. If it fails, little is said, and the venture capitalist is frequently blamed because they shut off the money tap. Success has a thousand parents, while failure is an orphan. Entrepreneurs have one common problem, the need for money.

Entrepreneurs quickly discover that, until they have money, a new venture is zilch, a figment of the imagination, and they are treading water.

Money is the fuel and life blood for every project. The search for startup dollars takes time, effort, money, and is frustrating far beyond expectations. There are no shortcuts, no quick fixes, and no guaranteed formula. The good news is that there are plodding Big Foot prints to follow which will enhance the chances of getting funded.

SOME COMMON TRUTHS

1. The entrepreneur must first accurately determine how much money is needed.
2. The entrepreneur most often assumes the role of a salesman in acquiring funding.
3. Investors invest in entrepreneurs, not companies.
4. Business goals and values must be shared with everyone.
5. Honesty is the prevailing policy.
6. Ask for what is needed.
7. Partners must share the same risk profile.
8. Partners will not be equals. Someone must drive the bus.
9. Institutional investment should be the last resort.
10. Lifestyle must not change when money is in the bank.

8

HOW TO TAKE STRESS, RISKS, FAILURES AND HARVEST AND MOVE ON

STRESS

A major Silicon Valley firm discovered that 50% of its employees declared stress to be a major problem for them. Other Valley firms report 80–90% of its employees have stress problems.

Studies portentiously estimate that stress costs U.S. firms about $150-billion a year. It is underscored by the fact that we consume more than $300-million worth of tranquilizers each year. A few years ago, the President's Commission on Mental Health estimated that one in four persons in the U.S. suffered from "severe emotional stress" without a diagnosable mental cause of physical illness! That supports the belief of many medical researchers that most diseases and illnesses are stress-related. Never mind that a handful of conceptual controversies persist, that experts cannot agree on what stress is precisely, exactly how it behaves, or what one course of action will control it. We know that stress does not produce pain or other warnings before doing severe damage. Yet stress is a major factor in high blood pressure, in strokes (all ages), heart attacks, coronary-artery diseases, drug abuse, and alcoholism. Stress also saps the immune system which it weakens and slows down.

Whatever one wants to call it, stress is part and parcel of every new venture.

Entrepreneurial stress is a product of tension caused by stressors. It is a biological state of alert that mobilizes the body to overcome a threat, real or perceived. The entrepreneural stressors are dynamic changes, niggling disappointments, constant frustrations, uncertainties, frenetic delays, little hassles, competitive upsets, unconfirmed rumors, company politics, ambiguities, lack of communications, personality clashes, and unresolved bits and pieces. To understand the nature of startup stress is critical. It is a potential problem of major proportions, and a new venture will go nowhere unless the entrepreneur can get a handle on stress. To ignore stress is to free fall without a parachute.

What is the Environment of Stress?

Stress is found in wars, uprisings, courtrooms, offices, crowds, noise, dirt, heat, smog, and, most particularly, in the uncertain environment of start-ups. Stress is a cunning predator and penetrates mahogany-paneled, air-conditioned, soundproofed, evergreen, deep pile, Muzak in the background, health-oriented buildings down to kitchen startup arenas. The entrepreneural environment is awash with high-octane startup achievers feverishly battling to get on the board with messianic zeal. This daft urgency is the incubator of stress which can permeate the entire firm from top to bottom. The belief is widely supported that:

Stress is self induced!

As startups emerge: conflict and unknown factors run rampant, options differ, holding one's tongue can be tension building, small pressures can be conpressing and erosive, choices constantly unclear, uncertainties shivery, working conditions demanding, and insecurity omnipresent. Entrepreneurs whip themselves to a frenzy to get ahead of the competitive pack, knowing the farther they get ahead, the greater the shafting. Work crises abound. The entrepreneur is as tight as a snare drum. The overstimulated body refuses to slow down and muscles become tighter and more cramped. Even when the threat disappears, the entrepreneur stays teetered on the edge, coiled hard, ready to spring on the next crisis. Stress can be insidious and not always hanging out in view for every entrepreneur. The business strategy veers to make a major crosscut due to the competitive environment or the product development. It is a new ball game. The company suddenly decides that it must pack up and move to Colorado, Georgia, Oregon, Arizona, Arkansas, Silicon Valley, Texas, or Idaho; in the middle of the semester or just after closing the deal on a too-expensive house.

After negotiating the startup hurdle, the next stress environment is rapid growth a high hurdle of challenges and frustrations.

As the tempo of startups accelerates, the entrepreneur faces greater uncertainty. The crises and pressures are more frequent and build up with intensity to reach deep into inner resources to respond. The knotted body finds it harder to react. In rapid growth, stress may flourish and, uncontrolled, can become a monkey on the back, creating more tension with each step. Stressors aggregate in new venture situations as the entrepreneur struggles to deal with the mincing problems, let alone the major ones. It can become the Chinese water torture. Water drips on the forehead, hour after hour and day after day. The entrepreneur can soon go Chop Suey. In summary, the environment of Big-*S* is widespread, self inflicted, and self sustaining. Stress is further exacerbated by the pioneering nature of the pursuit into the unknown, and stress does not top out until Harvest time.

Innovative Approaches to Stress Reduction

The typical stressed entrepreneur is a high-achiever, needs some completed events, and cannot tolerate being colloidally suspended in limbo for long. With the river-boat gambling ambience of startups, the arm wrestling pressures, and the hurly-burly pace of entrepreneurial workdays: it is small wonder another belief prevails that nothing can be done about stress in new ventures; it comes with the territory. "Stress is everywhere" is the doomsday siren's lilt. It is bad stuff and must happen. Little can be done and, *deja vu*, one should learn to live with stress, like bandy legs, bad knees, or a deviated septum. Yet, this is patently absurd! Something can be done!

The scoop that entrepreneurship and stress are inseparable and equal is pure boilerplate. As Sammy Davis sings, *it ain't necessarily so.*

Recent findings on the subject suggest cause for optimism. A crucial part of the story is that stress is what happens. The rest of the story is how we react to what happens. And how we respond is controlled by our minds and emotions. First, the first step is identify stress before it sets in and latches on. To ignore stress is to allow excessive stressors to build up as a creepy crawler, to grow into hypertension and end up as a silent killer. There are warning signals:

Tense business environment.
Little problems become big problems.
Easily ticked off.
Antsy.
Taking everyone's problems to heart.
Down in the dumps most of the day.
Junk food on the run, poor nutrition.
No goof-off time at the office.
Migraine headaches and sour stomach.
Lack of a regular exercise program.
No family time even when away from work.
Constant irritations at home.
Drinking to escape.
Smoking pot or using drugs to get relief.

Second, in stress reduction, an entrepreneur must be Teflon® coated, to allow the considerable strain and tension associated with a new venture to slough off and not stick in the craw. If the entrepreneur cannot muster a protective coating, stress can flub a good performance.

Third, stress will not quick-step away unless positive action is taken.

It is believed that stress can be shunted aside or even squeezed out. Big-S does not have to be a two-by-four constantly beating at our brains!

Fourth, a certain amount of stress is acceptable and productive. It can push us to perform at our best.

A prominent endocrinologist, Dr. Hans Selye says,

> "Most people who want to accomplish something,
> who are ambitious, live on stress; they need it."

Our perception of things determines how we will stand up to stress. Tension depends upon whether we make a mountain out of a molehill or a molehill out of a mountain. The following are needed:

Social support.   One must learn to become socially active. Leaning on the family, friends, and associates can help. Do not be afraid to lean on colleagues for a consoling hand. Share overloads, stress points, and management burdens.

Interaction.   Networking is to bounce options off on acquaintances, solicit inputs in planning, be garrulous, interact regularly, seek feedback, beckon approval, and subtly solicit honest opinions.

A definite advantage is a good memory for names. Write them down! The interactive and communicative person is accessible, optimistic, humble yet not obsequious, a yacker and a good listener, and lays off griping. Letting it all hang out is far better than stress smoldering inside. Subdued stress festers and clouds the entrepreneurial mind.

Nurturing.   Care about others. Be affectionate and receive love with humility. It is a two way street. Give of yourself. To care about others is to take a recess from stress.

Exercise.   Keep the body tuned. Exercise is an effective outlet for stress. Take aerobic walks instead of watching TV. Bike riding and jogging produces a rhythmic motion that tones the muscles and transfers psychological stress into more easily dealt with physical stress. Body surf. Pump iron. Yoga. About half an hour three times a week. Five minutes of seated or standing isometric exercises daily at the office can loosen tense muscles. Rotate the head and relax the neck muscles.

Relaxation.   A major key to warding off stress is the relaxation method instead of fight or flight.

A good method is practice meditation and relaxation. Take short breaks and grab catnaps.

Hobby lobby.   A hobby or recreation will divert stress. The best are unrelated to work and really fun. Spelunking, wind surfing, backpacking, stamp collecting, car restoring, furniture refinishing, scouting, orchid growing; are all great escapes and destressors.

Sleep.   The body's restoration system is sleep. Some need eight hours while others thrive on four hours. A sleep regimen that fits is important for resting one's body.

Abusing snoozing can induce stress and make an effective day's work impossible.

Powerful eating habits. Nutrition is the fuel to keep an entrepreneur pumped up. Stimulants in the form of junk food, black coffee, and candy bars create a breeding ground for stress.

Balancing food intake at lunchtime will insure formula one performance through the day.

Introduce into your munching habits raw veggies, fresh fruit, or sunflower seeds. After all, a well-stoked mind is one of the keys to entrepreneurial success.

You are what you eat:

- "No" to high-fat foods. Pass up steak, pork, lunch meats, and hard cheese.
- When peak performance is needed, nibble on a small light meal, bit of chicken, clear soup, or a light salad.
- If you work late, eat a hearty lunch; lean protein dishes, fresh fruit, raw veggies, high fiber foods.
- Do not start a business lunch with carbohydrates. Eat a roll after a low-fat protein such as fish.
- If you need a late-afternoon picker upper, think protein: granola bar, plain yogurt, raisins, cottage cheese, or hamburger (no bun).
- Need to calm down? Reach for carbohydrates: plain bagel, dry cereal, crackers. Eat with discretion.

Stress avoidance. Avoid stress-producing situations. Keep in mind that a confrontation is much less stressful than holding back with that gnawing worry, hidden anger, or harbored fear. If a stressful problem exists, try to tackle it in the first two hours of the day, when you are up and ready to go.

Procrastination. To push any task aside for later treatment is to invite stress. Management By Objectives (MBO) is a strongarm in reducing stress. As problems arise, do not pidgeonhole them for later action. Do it now!

Polyanna power. For everything that goes wrong there are probably ten or a hundred blessings. Dwell on the good things of life; ignore the bad.

Write it down. A small notebook *ist ein mussen*! Make it a habit to divide and classify. Refer to it often. If you do not put it on paper, it might be better to put it off!

Be long on stick-on notes. Such notations relieve the frustrated memory and reduces stress. But do not restructure your life to justify your notepad.

We have positive proof that stress exists in startups. Also, the fact that we are the masters of our own stressful destinies, and it does not have to be all that bad.

Remember, we bring stress on ourselves, and we possess the power to modify it to our advantage:

- Change your thinking. Stress control begins in the mind.
- Pick out two positives of each day. Forget the negatives.
- Learn to say "no." Too many "yeses" lead to stress.
- Fight insecurity. Boost your self esteem and self image.
- Waste time wisely. Doing nothing is sometimes A-OK.
- Plan for fewer interruptions. Do not get in the way of traffic.
- Slow down to a trot. It will get done, no big thing.
- Learn to giggle. Read the comics, listen to jokes, laugh.
- Smell the daisies. Learn to relax and meditate.
- Recharge your battery. Paperbacks, rock concerts, movies, theatre, barefoot in the park, toss frisbie, etc.
- Change your behavior. Dare to be different.

It is how we react that matters. To ignore stressful situations is to lead off with two strikes and will seriously influence the joy of doing.

RISKS

Though entrepreneurs have often been labeled as can-do persons who like to take risks, that is a fallacy. Entrepreneurs are saddled with risk, like it or not, and they do not like it.

Therefore, we should examine the subject of risk carefully. Our objective should be put into perspective. We must configure risk so as not to lurch episodically, wildly, and randomly within the innovative process.

The risk takers were the derring-doers of the last century with the railroads and steel mills. Now they are involved in million-dollar startups, billion-dollar takeovers, artificial heart transplants, biogenetic technology, space exploration, and other complex projects.

Barry Fischhoff said it simply,

> "You can't get through life without being a risk
> taker."

The notion that entrepreneurship and risk are intertwined is so seductive that it is not surprising that many try to sneak both into the tent.

Entrepreneurship and risk are side by side peas in a pod. They are simply live-ins.

To ignore risk, thinking what must be, will be, *que sera sera*, is pure bushwah.

Risk must be considered on its own merits and demerits. It can be dealt with singularly and separately. There is no unseverable umbilical cord.

Different risks get different titles and there is not even a repertoire of pedestrian responses.

At least five risks can face entrepreneurs:

1. Career. Entrepreneurship is a double jeopardy risk for one who has a job. Whether or not to jump ship and abandon a position with a firm is no pat decision. The risk is huge.

   For starters, it is the end of payday. There goes the budget! Also, we do not get a raincheck. It is also certain that the old job will be filled and unavailable for a return engagement.

   A larger question might be: will we be able to get another job at all? Those are two weighty risks.

2. Family. A commitment to entrepreneurship elbows the family aside. There will be little or no time for the family.

   A startup is a voracious time consumer; long hours and lost weekends as well. It does not care one whit about family relationships. The children. The spouse.

   In new ventures, the family unity is also on the line. Is it fair to ask the family to sacrifice security and take on a zany risk because the entrepreneur has been bitten by the startup bug?

   The divorce rate among entrepreneurs is sky high.

3. Personal. There is a gargantuan personal risk. The greater the commitment, the more the enterprise is internalized.

   On the upside, if the venture strikes it rich, the success may be attributed to causative factors now always to the entrepreneur. How could that one be missed?

On the down side, if the venture flops or goals are not reached, the critical finger will point to the entrepreneur as the villian.

Self esteem will be dragged through the mud. Feelings of guilt, shame, and degraded self image can be shattering. Once started, the process of self incrimination and the loss of confidence can throw one into a vicious spin.

4. Financial. Can the family coffers stand it? Every possession may be leveraged to the brim. The family will be compelled to go into low gear in spending, perhaps just above the poverty level. Will it hamper future personal financial security? What will happen if the start-up stumbles? Can the entrepreneur tolerate the risk? The entrepreneur could end up in enormous debt.

5. Investors. The entrepreneur has a very personal responsibility to investors for the seed money will probably come from family and close friends.

   Can they afford to invest the money? A larger question is, can they afford to lose money? How will they be paid back if the venture fails? They are investing in the entrepreneur more than the project. We risk friendships and kinships.

   George Orwell noted that money is the grand test of virtue!

   Beaucoup material has been handed out which does not address one salient fact in dealing with risk:

   Though risk exists, an entrepreneur can learn to
   cope.

It is one leg up to know that risk is not unmanageable but can even be turned to advantage! By the way, you better believe that risk is a strong motivator. Remember when William Tell was told by the tyrant that if he succeeded in knocking an apple off his sons's head with a bow and arrow on the first try, Tell would be pardoned. If he missed, he or the child would be killed. Will understood the risk he was taking. William Tell bowed and was true on the mark to the core. He sliced the apple in half.

Why do entrepreneurs take risks which can shackle them for the future while others are content to lead more plebian existences? Because there are a lot of people who are willing to risk all for a small bit of glory.

Consider the Suez Canal, first built about 2000 BC by the Egyptians to connect the Red Sea to the Mediterranean. Attempts to rebuild it had been undertaken by the Pharoah Necho, Darius the Great of Persia, the Roman Emperor Trajan, Harun Al-Raschid, the Caliph of Baghdad, the Republic of Venice, and Napoleon. All without success. The probability of accomplishing the task was so far out and the risks so enormous, everyone else gave up. Gutsy Ferdinand de Lesseps took it on. Ferdie raised the capital by hook or by crook. How he overcame the problems and barriers is mind-boggling, but he pushed the project to completion by 1869. It was the dizzy ultimate of risk taking, like walking a high wire in go-aheads. Fortunately, Ferdinand was not aware of the enormity of the insane risk.

Why did Ferdie to it?

It could be explained by Fast Eddie Felson as he balanced a chalked cue stick in the smoky pool hals of "The Hustler,"

> "You make shots that nobody's ever made before.
> And you play the game the way nobody's ever play-
> ed it before."

It is right on target! The motivation is as obvious as Cyrano's nose. It is like listening to Andrew Grove or Peter Ueberroth or Jerry Saunders jawboning about what makes them tick.

The message is loud and clear. Just do not ignore risk. It will not blow away. Evaluate it, understand it, and deal with it.

FAILURE

The high rates of new venture failures must be given the attention they deserve for we know that failure has much to teach, not only to those who failed but to others about to enter the ring.

This is not to say that all failures need to be eliminated. A certain iteration of failure is part of what Joseph Schumpeter describes as, "creative self destruction."

But that is not the case. Failure is an integral part of the dynamics of innovation and economic renewal.

Failure also has a social value, if an ignoble one. Were every single new venture to make it big, the entrepreneurial world would be inhabited only by success. It would be a relentlessly boring environment. Whom then would we have to leer at disparagingly? As the phrase goes:

"It is not enough that I succeed. My friends must fail
also."

Students of intellectual thought know that this is only half a joke and
half a truth. For a time, failure in entrepreneurship was a crushing disgrace.
It was a humiliating and embarrassing situation.

John Keats wrote,

"There is not a fiercer hell than failure in a great
object."

It was commonly believed that failure cast doubt not only on a person's
business acumen but on character and even morality. The statistics on
failures are ominous. About one out of ten makes it to the success podium
while two or three fall into apoplectic failure immediately. Henry Ford had
two failures. J.C. Penney failed several times. Nolan Bushnell said Pizza
Time Theater would open 1,000 outlets in a few years. It filed for bankruptcy. Bushnell's Atari teetered and failed, to be resurrected by Jack
Tramiel. Do not forget Gene Amdahl, father of the IBM 360. He did not
make it with Amdahl Computer or Trilogy. Adam Osborne went down
with the Osborne Computer. Mike Hollis's high flying Air Atlanta hit the
tarmac not long ago. They, and many other entrepreneurs, who experienced failure, saw the future through rose tinted glasses. They painted a
beautiful picture of what they were going to do, but the cards stacked
against them. They chased their startup towards doomsday, often believing
the turnaround was just over the next hill. They found it difficult to admit
that it was a "MAYDAY," that "enough was enough." In many cases, the
shareholders or the board of directors could only get the founders out of
the door by court order, for not many venture creators admit failure without
a fight.

Psychologist Kathleen Lynch explains in a published article:

"To be an entrepreneur, you almost have to not be
able to face possible failure. It's an organizational
equivalent of a person recognizing that he has a
terminal disease."

Failure does not always hit the fan immediately. Many marginal startups
wallow, huff and puff between success and failure. They are failures in the

making but do not know it. They walk trudgingly, not run, in the muck and mire of mediocrity and suddenly, one day, they are gone.

In Ernest Hemingway's *The Sun Also Rises*, Mike Campbell spoke about how failures occur,

> "Two ways. Gradually and then suddenly."

The lessons derived from being engaged in the process of failing can provide a solid base for avoiding the disappointment of failure on the next go around or the guilt pangs of unattained goals. The genre of failure has come about in the last few years—for so many entrepreneurs have failed, stood up, brushed themselves off, and climbed up the Jacob's ladder to enormous heights.

Failure is no longer shameful because of the uncontrollable nature of new ventures. Clearly, the failure of a startup no longer means the failure of a venture career either. The rate of success of second tries at entrepreneurship are almost double those who have not experienced failure. Many entrepreneurs have reckoned that lessons from failures are an essential part of the learning process in gaining an entrepreneurial apprenticeship. That is why failure should be studied with the same inquiry as success.

All failures are:

1. Uncontrollable
2. Controllable
3. Incremental

Uncontrollable

Poor timing, bad luck, economics, and competition are key causative factors in uncontrollable failures.

Markets are chancy. Luck is flighty. Economics are unpredictable. Competitive response is a potpourri of whimsey. Though the above four factors are typically uncontrollable, there is an important parallel issue. Crucial to a failure outcome is how the entrepreneur deals with it. That is to say, failure is unpredictable, if not uncontrollable, but the second part to the equation is response.

Not all negative signals are causes to pick up the marbles and run. But when? How? Ah, that is the rub! We can control the impact of impending failure by catching the signals early on and taking corrective action.

In some cases, the direction can be changed, and a new venture even turned around to survive. In other cases, the project may be positively a lost cause and it is time to salvage what can be saved.

Two skilled business authors, Jerry Ross and Barry Staw, expressed it accurately when they wrote,

> "Good management consists of knowing when to
> call it quits."

The pivotal signals in uncontrollable failures are twofold. One, the four factors are random and, two, damage can be reduced by making quick fixes expeditiously. The sweet spots, then, are recognition and response.

Controllable

Management By Ignorance (MBI) is the most common affliction in controllable failures.

Unfortunately, MBI is a future behavior and not apparent in the enthusiastic piecing of a startup management team. It is in implementation that management choices may not translate into effective decision-making.

Examining the new venture horizon at any given time reveals a number of firms ensnarled in the business equivalent of startup flypaper; bad products or shoddy markets they cannot shake quickly or gracefully.

The harder they try, the more firmly stuck entrepreneurs become. They become trapped in what failure researchers describe as "escalation dilemmas." The stubborn entrepreneur continues to pour effort and money into the "big picture," imprudently throwing good after bad. Worse than businesses flat out going under is the tragic drama which unfolds when short-fall signals begin to appear, and no one pays any mind. Equally unfortunate is when a testy problem is recognized but is identified wrongly.

Buckminster Fuller spent the last fifty years of his life delivering an urgent message,

"Humans have learned only through mistakes. The billions of humans in the course of history have had to make quadrillions of mistakes . . . The courage to adhere to the truth as we learn it involves, then, the courage to face ourselves with the clear admission of all the mistakes we have made. Mistakes are sins only when not admitted."

Remember the airline pilot who announced to the passengers,

> "The bad news is that we are lost. But—the good
> news is that we are making good time."

Some entrepreneurs are like that. They speak good news in sepulchural tones and ignore the bad. They do not know that the play is over until the sheriff drops the fire curtain. In *The Wall Street Journal*, a CPA noted that seat-of-the-pants managers frequently fail to monitor all aspects of the business. They have not the faintest clue of the little picture.

Everything comes up roses if sales are increasing, and they are not overdrawn at the bank; forgetting the payables in the drawer and myriad warning flags waving frantically. Disbelief caroms off the blackboard when unpaid bills are taken to the cash register and the currency clamp rests on fluff.

Many entrepreneurs seem to have a predilection for failure and invariably twist triumph into disaster. Instead of profiting from a great venture capital opportunity, Christopher Columbus died in poverty and dispair. He could have had more than just a town in Ohio, a street in San Francisco, and a day of celebration named after him. In his success he really flopped. He failed because he did not know how to handle the golden ring of success.

But how about Thomas Crapper, who invented the toilet? He should have been flush but died a pauper. Then there was Ben Franklin. If he had succeeded in exploiting his kite flying, Pennsylvanians would be paying Con Franklin!

It is difficult to forget the doctor who reported to the family that the operation was a success but the patient died. His was an oxymoronic interpretation of failure.

Incremental

The bulk of startups rest in the middle range between success and failure. They shuffle along aimlessly and do not approach stated objectives. Yet they do not quantify as failures. They are amiable nonentity ventures, living dead, that walk in place, going nowhere.

Investors put money into a startup with specific, measureable return on investment expectations. An investor's view is apt to be that if a new venture does not meet investment forecasts, it is a failure. Unfortunately, almost half of new ventures do not reach stated revenue/profit goals. That is why venture capitalist Hal Nissley takes entrepreneur intended goals and subtracts 50%. Some entrepreneurs have a focus maintenance tic. They have a short interest span and cannot turn down new opportunities. At first blush, an opportunity is so enticing, so challenging, and so alluring. They just cannot keep their eyes on the ball. When a new opportunity appears, they are swinging. The chase is so attractive, they drop what they are doing and take on every new opportunity dropped at their doorstep. If it is analyzed with complete detachment, it is no more than a seductive siren using wily ways to pull an entrepreneur off of the charted course. Many entrepreneurs have failed because they could not resist an opportunity and chased every new one with a butterfly net. In summary, we can categorize failures in a host of ways, from the bully successes to the consumate failures with the bulk of mini-failures hovering in between.

Dealing with failure:

1. Bury failure.
   Do not mourn.
   It is ancient history.
   Know now what can be done and what cannot be done.
   Start again! A little smarter, a little wiser.
2. Accept the gaff.
   Do not pass the buck.
   Accept the blame and take the gaff.
   Success starts with a clean slate.
   It may be painful, but that is the first step in emerging from failure.
3. Listen hard to past lessons.
   An in-depth analysis of the reasons for failure will reap enormous benefits.
   It is important to recap the past events objectively.
   Learn to learn.
   A failure unexamined remains a failure forever.
4. Maintain a positive attitude.
   Attitude is almighty.
   No matter what happens, keep a happy face.
   It is infectious and confidence building.
   People migrate to positive personalities.
   Positivity is beautiful, negativism is blah.
5. Keep a bright light shining in the window.

Make tracks and distance from the failure.
Imagine what it will all look like ten years from now.
The future is sunny and bright.
Dream of far-off places and things.
6. Be open to new ideas.
   After failure, new startup opportunities become more quantifiable
   because of experiential data and thus, more achievable.
   Continue to sweep for ideas.
   Keep all options open.
7. Make a strategic move.
   Knowing the project has failed is not enough.
   To turn from a flop to a hit requires doing.
   Give yourself a pat on the back for having made the effort.
   Remember that the one failure does not a loser make.
   Get the show on the road.

It is doubtful that any entrepreneur ever really succeeded without being able to deal with failure.

Strange as it may seem, if we have the guts to slough off personal rejection, failure to meet objectives, guilt, wasted effort, even psychological defeat should our startup fail we have taken a giant step in the pursuit of success.

Boxing impressario Don King said it well,

> "When things begin to fall apart, I think, 'Don, you've been here before, and you can handle whatever comes out of the trees or from under the rocks.'"

Success is even sweeter the next time around for those who show the appropriate response to failure. Rather than an apologia, entrepreneurs should take it on the chin, move out, and this time, score a knockout.

Don King counsels boxers if they lose a championship match,

> "Dare to be great again . . . Remember, you grow through loss. Let's regroup and make victory rise like a Phoenix from defeat."

Al Copeland's brother gave him a franchise for Tastee-Donuts. He worked hard and watched the chicken people at Kentucky Fried Chicken (KFC) across the street. They worked 8 hours instead of his 12–14 hour days and made twice as much money. He decided that he could not make it with Tastee-Donuts and worked hard to piggyback KFC. He created a spicy Cajun recipe and opened up Popeye's Fried Chicken. It is a walloping success!

Al said,

> "If I went bust tomorrow, I could make a million
> in a year starting from scratch."

That is a willingness to admit a mistake, take a stop/loss, and to move on, post haste; the kind of two-fisted determination to overcome the obstacles and odds. Such a fighting spirit is common to robust comebacks.

One shiny day Ron Berger was worth more than $5 million. He was expecting $3 million in VC funds. Not only did the money not materialize but the bank called his loan of $1.2 million! The dreary next day, no banker would lend him a plug nickel. His hallowed new venture, the Photo Factory, headed for the barn and Chapter XI bankruptcy. Without missing a beat, Ron started a new venture. He fought his way back up. More than 660 people have opened franchises under his company, National Video, making it one of the largest video chains in the world!

Earl "Madman" Muntz remained on the leading edge of retail technology for fifty years, making and losing dozens of fortunes.

Two of them would have earned Oscars: the $73 million he pulled in by 1940 as the world's largest used car dealer (WWII made the business unprofitable) and the $55 million he earned ten years later selling black and white TV sets (RCA invented color and killed the deal). Muntz went from boom to bust with all-aluminum houses and a school of charm. Recently, a Muntz venture became one of California's leading dealers of satellite equipment; the business clears over $20-million a year.

Activision's Levy views failure as a valuable test of mettle:

> "The mark of a person's character is how he deals
> with adversity, not success. But failure has a way of
> handing out lessons that stick with entrepreneurs
> and, in the best of circumstances, actually strength-
> ens them."

Jesse Aweida bounced back with Aweida Systems Corporation less than a year after his startup, Storage Technology, filed for Chapter XI bankruptcy amid a flurry of suits. He advises:

> "Once a calamity is upon you, the worst thing you
> can do is nothing. Just go back to work and do it
> better the second time."

The route to victory is one of sheer perserverance. Perceive each defeat not as a dead end but a brief detour on an upward path.

Entrepreneurial professor Jeffrey Timmons said,

> "Failure is fire and heat that tempers steel. It's a
> wonderful Darwinian mechanism that sorts out the
> promoter and get-rich-quick artists from resilient en-
> trepreneurs who create value."

Success is always waiting on the far side of failure!

In conclusion, the major toehold on entrepreneurship in this country is monotheistic. Worship is at the altar of one god—success. Failure is relegated to the pews. Corporations avidly pay hordes of motivational gurus to get pumped up with upbeat, inspirational messages. They pony up money for enough can-do books to ruin a few forests. We spend precious little time trying to analyze startups that went bellyup, even though more than half of them were less than five years old. Yet the bottom line is that understanding the nature and causes of failures is almost as essential as the how, whys, and wherefores of success.

IBM's Thomas Watson had a formula worth noting:

> "Double your rate of failure. Failure is a teacher—
> a harsh one, but the best."

His attitude was that success merely encourages repetition of old behavior whereas failure is educational because it inspires change.

HARVEST

To nurture and grow a new venture until enough value has been added to permit a harvesting opportunity is what entrepreneurship is all about.

There are three harvesting scenarios:

Ignored

When a new venture is in the embryonic stage, harvesting is so distant it is often ignored. An intense feeling of my-baby and parenting exists. The immediate goal is scaling the mountain, not where are we going to put the flag when we get to the top. To discuss future harvesting strategies appears far fetched and presumptuous. If the firm evolves according to the business plan or surpasses its objectives, the entrepreneur is concerned with managing growth, finances, and the future. Harvesting would be tantamount to abandonment! It would be awful, cowardly, and the subject matter pure pap. Harvest planning in the seminal stages simply sits low on the priority totem pole. But it should not.

Imperative

Harvesting under ordinary conditions is complex. Under duress, it can be catastrophic and out of control. Without notice, harvesting may be forced on a company as a result of a sudden windshear of luck, timing, competition, or economics. A new technology appears out of nowhere. A Big Blue, IBM-like, brings its massive resources to bear to wipe out an itchy upstart. A market fades away. Key management abandons ship to go with a major competitor. A recession puts a kibosh on sales. As it all hits the fan, it may get so bad that a company may have to sell out at a bargain-basement price, merge with a takeover firm, or be put on the sales block. The founders are helpless. Harvesting by imperative leaves no room for strategizing or maximizing.

Planned

Harvesting is scoretime. It is the Big Payoff, the bottom line for investors. Harvesting demands thought, anticipation, and planning for a desired outcome.

To plan when, if, and how to harvest the capital gain value is critical to the entrepreneur hero.

When. The startup must have created adequate added value. It is up to the company or the entrepreneur to decide when the value has reached heights high enough for the founders to successfully reap a harvest.

The added value must be realistically attractive.

A strong track record has to be established to appear to the public offering market. Investors will not buy on the "come" alone. The new offering must exude confidence that the enterprise is on the roll and has much farther to go.

The present value added must be there and the future is the carrot to entice the offering buyers.

If. The if decision is a big one. There is pride and accomplishment in the growing company. Perhaps the founders are happy with the situation as it is tooling along.

There is also relatively comfortable management and reporting. Harvesting is not an imperative but an option and with it comes problems.

They may not want to take on the burden of conversion and attendant hassling.

Working as they are, the money founders earn may be adequate for their needs. Should they take the added value out of the company by cashing the chips or leave it in as equity (there is a risk)?

Many choices bubble up: chuck it all, take the money, restore old Jaguars, play golf, stay where we are, go public, sell out, and other alternatives.

To harvest also means giving up identity! Power!

The investors were promised a harvest, an opportunity to recoup their investments, and make a bundle.

There is also a social purpose for a new enterprise which is worthy of a harvest.

Harvesting implies expansion. It means technological innovation, new jobs, consumers, investment, and economic health. It boosts tax income for the community, city, state, and government. Expanding is for the social good.

Nevertheless, it is up to the founders, if or if not.

How. This is a testy question. There are six principal ways to harvest:

1. Going Public.

   Not many firms find it attractive to go public.

   It costs time and money. Lots of both.

   Management flexibility is constrained.

   The Securities Exchange Commission (SEC) governs consumes time, and is restrictive.

Substantial additional costs in government reporting and responsibilities to shareholders ensue.

The founders may not realize a financial gain for years after the Initial
Public Offering (IPO).

2. Selling Out.

Many believe this is the route to follow.

Often the acquiring firm will demand the founder team remain in a
long-term management contract.

Cash can have tax consequences whereas stock may result in a
tax-free exchange (with risk).

The entrepreneur loses control.

Bye-bye lots of tax benefits: credit card, car, etc.

3. Merging.

Merger with another company is another method for founders to
come out ahead.

Some cash and stock are usually held in the combined firm.

Long term employment and/or consulting contracts may be part of
the deal.

Be prepared for the combined company not to do as well as the sum
of the two parts.

4. Management Leveraged Buy Out (LBO).

Selling to existing management or partners is often a viable decision.

Rarely will money be up front.

LBOs can be fragile and are vulnerable to erosion.

Buyers always want to extend the payout period whereas the seller
wants to shorten it.

Better to reduce the price and get some cash.

5. Employee Buyout—Employee Stock Ownership Plan (ESOP).

The ESOP plan is often used in closely held firms.

Pension plan funds and future earnings form the basis for an ESOP
buyout.

ESOP is no guarantee the company will succeed.

6. Milking The Cash Cow.

With robust profit margins, it is possible that the firm will throw off
more cash than the entrepreneur and founders can spend.

Milking the cash cow restricts growth and bleeds cash out of the
company.

It is a short term strategy.

Harvest goal-setting acknowledges a long-term objective to create value added in the new venture and discusses harvest alternatives of the added value. Such planning is expressed in the elasticity of expectations when future rates of change are expected to equal current rates of change in the scenario. The validity and usefulness of the first thrust at a harvest strategy may be zilch, but the probability of using it fits into the same category. It may be highly futuristic and imprecise but that is not to be minded. As the startup goes through growth phases, permutations take place, and the harvesting plan begins to be kneaded to fit present reality. The viability increases with permutations until the harvesting strategy makes sense and is attainable. If upgraded wisely, the harvesting strategy and reality soon go hand in hand.

It is too early to know whether or not certain factors are useful or accurate, for no significant measurements can be made without data. This assumes *ceteris paribus*, that all other things are equal. As the new venture evolves, kneading and modifying the harvesting strategy will increase its veritability and the probability of success. In addition, not all added value can be converted in a harvest. That is why it is important to have a handle on the amount of the added value and its convertibility. Also, the amount of value added in terms of capital gain measurably raises the choices as compared to those new venture which have little added value.

Though there are no simple solutions, blessed are the erected signposts and warning lights that can offer a strategic basis for dealing with a harvest. When Richard Ferris took over United Air Lines, each share of stock was worth about $22. He later had a falling out and left the company. The firm split into profit components for harvesting. The value created was over $100 per share!

Ken Ellred begat *Inmac*, a computer supply magazine. After about four years, enormous value was created. He had a harvesting plan. It was tenuous and constantly changed. The time to harvest came, and the company want to a public offering. Ellred and the founders emerged with tens of millions of dollars, yet still remained in control of the firm. The company has continued its upward trend in a robust fashion.

Fred Gibbons had a similar experience at Software Publishing. He ended up with about a $20 million harvest and still maintains a strong stock position. However, Fred is still active with the company, which provides him with as much money as he needs. The $20 million is sitting in the bank. Was it a good move to harvest? The jury is still out.

Here are some wise observations:

- Put a harvest strategy in the plan.
- Initial harvesting plans are not set in granite.
- Timeframe from start to harvest is 3–5 years.
- Happiness is cash in the bank.
- Never, never, never turn down an offer without a look-see.
- An opportunity usually passes by once.
- Happiness is cash in the bank.
- Hanging in there can be dangerous.
- Going for more than the added value is chewing bubble gum.
- Happiness is cash in the bank.
- Harvest when it is not necessary.
- Harvesting can mean family time.
- Life can be beautiful after harvesting.
- Happiness is cash in the bank.

The difference between harvesting a new venture with a harvest plan in place and harvesting with little or no preparation, is so diverse that there is no serious conflict in which to do.

MOVE ON

Once a new venture has been pulled "through the harvest knothole," to use Webster's term, the remaining question is moving on.

The purpose of harvesting is to capitalize on added value. This is a tradeoff of ownership for capital. Hopefully, the added value will be large enough for the entrepreneur to reap a substantial harvest.

There is a new ball game. The bloom is off the rampaging upstart. The burgeoning company is a burgeoned company. Outside investors have acquired a share of ownership in the firm. It calls for a change in management style. How much power will the entrepreneur be allowed, which Henry Kissinger refers to as "the ultimate aphrodisiac," is a moot question.

The harvested environment is antithetical to the nature of free-swinging entrepreneur heroes. That is why, by and large, commitment to a harvest presupposes a change or a decision to move on. This, of course, may not include businesses which depend upon specific technical skills of the entrepreneur or in some family-owned businesses. The entrepreneur is faced with several choices: one, to wind down; two, to hang in there; three, to move on. When entrepreneurs opt to wind down they may stay on to make an orderly transition. It is not often as smooth as advertised but works in the interest of both the new venture and the entrepreneur.

If the founder chooses to hang in there, it may be because he/she is able to maintain stock control. This option has various outcomes. It is only a happy one if the entrepreneur is capable of adapting to a new role. Though many think they can, most find it a road full of chuckholes. The typical entrepreneur hero finds the loose, stimulating challenges gone. That is why the preferred route is to follow the advice which comes from the title of a Woody Allen movie;

"Take the money and run."

Moving on must not be a knee jerk reaction. It should be a preplanned scenario woven onto the harvest so that when the harvest has been completed, the decision can be implemented with grace.

Unintentionally, the Beatles provided a musical theme for moving on, in their song, "Hello, Goodbye."

"You say goodbye, and I say hello. I wonder why
you say goodbye and I say hello?"

The signature of hello, goodbye is when the harvest is over. Most move on to other things, such as the following:

- Entrepreneurs often take up civic endeavors. They contribute money and time to a variety of worthwhile civic and community projects.
- Some entrepreneurs return to their roots. They buy a farm, ranch, or orchard and get back to the good earth.
- Other entrepreneurs move on gently by downsizing. They stay on the Board of Directors, remain as a consultant, or as an advisor for a few years. They become executives emeritus.
- Some entrepreneurs chase lost opportunities. They bask in the sun, get their handicap down, or fish out get bored, and decide to try

to do it all over again. They recall seeing opportunities flash by when in the throes of their startup. The chase is on again.

- Some see moving on as a recapture of the family. During entrepreneurship, the household was a one-parent dwelling. Now the entrepreneur can be at home in the daytime! Robert Frost describes home as, "Where, when you have nowhere to go, they have to take you in." It is a time to enjoy the fruits of harvesting.
- Financial expectations must be reasonable. There may be stock sale limitations. It may take some time to cash out. By the time all of the bills are paid, taxes are reconciled, there may not be the vast amount anticipated. But that is not bad. Grin all the way to the bank.
- Moving on is not the end. It may be the start of something new, as the song goes.
- Entrepreneurs usually become busier than ever. They get as active in other things as when they were first involved in the earlier stages.

Moving on can result in a happy outcome by planning the moves—to be prepared as a good scout. This kind of thinking also facilitates getting good replacements as it offers a future.

The first step is to understand the options. How it will be done should be a miniplan. It will cut down on dissension, conflict, and uncertainty. After a transition time, the entrepreneur can carefully turn over the reins to the new management in an orderly fashion. It is likely that the entrepreneur will have to give up the oval office and move on to a smaller one. This is symbolic as well as in the interest of effective management.

It is a common practice to keep one's secretary for the period of time though that may jeopardize his/her continuing as executive secretary to the president.

The office can be maintained for no more than a few months. The entrepreneur cannot continue indefinitely to hang on for it will surely cause friction. The entrepreneur should always be available for consultation and support, when asked. No criticism of management is allowed. No second-guessing is permitted while on the premises. Hours should be on a declining basis.

On the flip side, outside activities can be on the rise: sports, hobbies, community participation, and trips with the family.

It is important to clearly understand that the decision to harvest is also an acknowledgement that some part or all of management perogitives will be given up, that a new and more formal style of reporting and accountability will take place, that the old agenda is no longer applicable.

The environment will not be an entrepreneurial one and the entrepreneur who harvests cannot have it both ways: to keep the company and take the loot.

The entrepreneur will soon find out that by hanging around means to be left out of the mainstream. It is humiliating and a further incentive to move on.

SOME COMMON MYTHS

1. The company cannot survive without me.
2. Staying on will be the same as before.
3. Moving on is to oblivion.
4. Staying on will ensure power and identity.
5. The smaller the harvest, the less the need to move on.
6. Tomorrow will be the same as today.
7. Goal setting can be after the harvest.
8. It is not possible to do it again.
9. Do not be frivolous.
10. The security guard will never ask for my identification card.

SOME UNCOMMON TRUTHS

1. Successful movers had an agenda.
2. Realistically appraise skills and goals.
3. Know that you will be missed, not needed.
4. Criticizing usually turns out to be a boomerang.
5. Believe that you will find happiness in the great beyond.
6. Pre-test moving on by reducing responsibility, authority, and accountability.
7. Start golfing, fishing, or whatever before harvesting, not after moving on.
8. Moving on offers a new world of opportunity.

9. Have dreams and pursue them!
10. Moving on can be a blast, if you believe it. Have fun!

9

BLOCKBUSTERS FOR THE HIGH ROAD TO SUCCESS

GOING ALL THE WAY

Motivation, mission, strategy, mobility, passion, tenacity, urgency, and fulfillment are the blockbusters for boosting up to go all the way.

Motivation is clearly the dominant factor. It is the driving force, that irrepressible urge to achieve.

Debbi Fields was in her early twenties when she started her famous chocolate-chip cookie business. Highly motivated, she said,

> "Be the best you can be. Whatever you do, do it because you love it, not because of the money. Remember that what you do must benefit your customer."

Mission is a total commitment to the task. Partial commitment or playing-it-safe does not work. David Seuss worked for the Boston Consulting Group. To start Spinnaker Software meant giving up a $125,000-a-year job. David made the cut. He was highly mission-oriented, and Seuss succeeded!

Strategy is the plan for getting to the top of the mountain. William Shakespeare wrote, "Determine on some course, more than a wild exposure to each chance."

Mobility means doing it. Until the entrepreneur is mobile and an action is taken, there is nothing.

IBM's Thomas Watson observed,

> ". . . the worst thing we could do would be to lie dead
> in the water . . ."

Passion is an enthusiasm, zeal, and joy for entrepreneuring. John Templeton, chairman of the highly successful Templeton Growth Fund wrote,

> "Live your life as if it were an exciting challeng-
> ing, ongoing, spiritual adventure."

Tenacity means bulldogging ahead, fast-forward and no reverse. No matter what, the entrepreneur presses onward. Bob Steinborn, the co-founder of Chicago Brother's Pizza, gives his advice:

> "Never give up! Continue forward, even though
> you may have some rough times; persevere."

Urgency is a restlessness and a compelling desire to get the job done—now! Jerry Greenfield is a co-founder Ben & Jerry's Ice Cream. Jerry is an urgent and restless person with a compelling desire to get the job done. Jerry noted,

> "The best advice I received was from (my partner)
> Ben Cohen. He said, 'When somebody tells you that
> something can't be done, all it really means is that it
> hasn't been done before.'"

Favorable situational conditions are critical in providing an opportunistic environment for the entrepreneur. Situational conditions are often convertible, frequently irrational, such as luck and timing. It is the exploiter who makes, the one who recognizes the situation. Good or bad, many unfavorable situations can be enhanced, altered, and reversed.

Dick Melman is the founder of Ed Debevic's restaurants. He has been a restaurant entrepreneur of unusual success. His advice is,

> "You need knowledge, you need money, and you
> need to love what you are doing. If you are missing
> one of those ingredients, (starting a business) is very
> difficult. If you are missing two of the ingredients,
> you have got to be crazy!"

IDEAS

Idea formulation is a product or service with a target market in mind and
a plan to satisfy that opportunity sensibly.

Research in the formulation of an idea is the initial step, remembering
that research is two-faced. It is a mask/face phenomenon which the Japanese refer to as "omote" which means in front, *de jure*, the mask, that
which appears outwardly. "ura" refers to behind, *de facto*, the true face, or
the real life. Basic research can validate a concept while extended research
may invalidate it. There are so many variables and uncertainties, real and
perceived, pluses and minuses, knowns and unknowns that research must
be evaluated correctly. There have been startups that stood up well in the
initial research. Extended research was continued in the guise of being
more thorough and began to cast doubt on the initial studies. Soon, so
much data were collected as to validate the way the entrepreneur wanted
to go, and to deny almost any decision.

Of course we want the relevant facts. But there is a point of diminishing
return in continued research. The signals begin to get redundant, cluttered,
mixed, misleading, and contradictory. Therefore, research must be tempered with knowing "what it really means" and when "enough is enough."
There comes a time when the entrepreneur has to pull the plug, get off the
dime, and get going—no matter what. The real estate developer, James
Rouse, tells of his very successful Faneuil Hall project. Many developers
researched and researched the rehabilitation job and gave it a thumbs
down. He said,

> "Nobody would come in to do that project. We
> didn't have sense enough to know it couldn't be
> done—thank goodness!"

So they plunged ahead to success!

Idea mobilization is as important as idea formulation.

Entrepreneur dreamers and schemers outnumber entrepreneur doers.

POSITIVE THINKING

Positive thinking is a valuable tool in the quest for the golden grail. It is a can-do attitude that can be learned! Art Linkletter, Drs. Bob Schuller, Bill Appleton, Irene Kassoria, and Gary Emery are advocates of the positive thinking ethic. They agree with Dr. Norman Vincent Peale:

> "Believe in yourself! Have faith in your abilities!
> Without a humble but reasonable confidence in your
> own powers you cannot be successful or happy."

All are successes and enthusiastically endorse Dr. Peale's gospel that positive thinking is the key to open doors, to moving and shaking, accomplishment, and joy in life. They were all able to put wings to their latent powers through positive thinking and soar to sky levels of success. Through the power of positive thinking, entrepreneurs can accomplish remarkable goals.

Bob Haft founded Crown Books. He said,

> "Listen, dream, study, experiment, tinker, and excel."

GO FOR IT!

New ventures come in every size, shape, and form to fit a dream. Small is the most beautiful of all. Even if a billion-dollar-a-year market is on the long-range horizon, it makes sense to start small.

There are supporting reasons for thinking smaller than bigger:

- More smaller venture opportunities exist than bigger ones.
- A small startup is less complicated. It fits the KISS principle, "Keep It Simple Stupid!"
- On the wee side offers greater chances of funding.

- The entrepreneur can keep a larger piece of the pie.
- The returns may be smaller but the risks are less.
- Statistics show a higher rate of success in small startups than in large ones.
- Small can make a startup less onerous emotionally.
- Happiness is measured by accomplishment and not only by dollars. Small increases the probability.

Stanford business Professor Steven Brandt urges,

> "Start cheap, small, and local. That keeps your mistakes survivable and your customer feedback loops rapid and accurate."

PAPER THE IDEA

Commit the idea to foolscap. The miniplan should tell the story. It should show confidence, honesty, guarded enthusiasm, and accuracy. The targets must be reasonable and, if the numbers come up too robust, lean a little to the conservative side. Al Copeland started Popeye's Famous Fried Chicken and Biscuits. He said,

> "Plan for what happens when you succeed and plan for what happens if your fail. Planning is the most important thing."

DESCRIBE THE PRODUCT, SERVICE, OR WHATEVER

The product, service, or whatever must be clearly described. The entrepreneur should estimate how long it will take for prototype development, associated costs, and a fully-allocated-cost selling price. What does it take to get it from the drawing board to market?

Describe it in simple detail. What is what Venture Capitalist Arthur Rock refers to as the "unfair" advantage? Why is this better than what is on the market? Where will it be manufactured? How will it be produced?

Remember, the entrepreneur is telling what time it is, not how to build a watch! Too much detail can be gagging and cause an irrepressible ennui. Few investors have adequate technical backgrounds to understand sophisticated engineering embroidery.

UNDERSTAND THE MARKET FULLY

A definable need must exist in the niche market. According to Maslow's Heirarchy of Needs, needs are physiological, safety-oriented, social, self-esteem-oriented, and self-actualization-oriented. We all have need lists. However, need alone is not enough to get a product off the shelves. The key is a market demand which will move the product. Often elegant products are developed for which a need exists but not a market demand.

A market demand contains three components;

1. Need,
2. Ability to buy, and
3. Willingness to buy.

The marketing whiz, James McManus, said it wisely,

> "It's not an issue of whether you can make it, it's whether you can sell it."

This supports a paradigm for memory etching:

> Products do not create demand. Demand creates products.

THE MARKET NICHE IS EVERYTHING

The total market must be understood as well as the market niche in which the product or service will be distributed. Entrepreneurs must know the market niche size, characteristics, and response mechanisms in order to serve the niche competitively. R. David Thomas is the founder of Wendy's. "Know who your customers are," he said. "Know who they are, the type of people they are, and always remember that you're in business for your customers. Whatever you do must benefit your customers."

The entrepreneur who matches enterprise to niche is certain of success for niche-matching is everything! Forecasting niche behavior is really a snow job but cannot be ignored. Imbedded in every market is constant change. We may identify the past behavior of a niche, how it acts now, but future behavior is something else. To forecast change is far from easy. To evaluate future life in a niche is difficult though necessary.

To be a creative "nicher" is to look ahead. The floppy disk entrepreneur who drives into the future while looking in the rear view mirror is a thinker.

NETWORK ALL OVER THE PLACE

Value all comments and talk with everybody. Listen! Come out of the closet. Try it on for size with family and friends, at the dinner table or anywhere. Mach Schoenfeld brought samples of his new yogurt kind of product, Tootje, to a Bible class for tasting. He avidly noted responses on a notepad.

Former New York Mayor Ed Koch is an inveterate networker and market sampler. He quizzes anyone who will answer on a multitude of subjects, as if he had a patent on networking.

Coalition building provides a valuable source of information. Most businesses are people businesses, so it is important to build a constituency. Useful suggestions will emerge from the most unexpected sources, so be more listener than talker.

GET THE MANAGEMENT TEAM ON LINE

Initially, a startup is a one person band. Everything is done solo, *a capella*, solitaire. The entrepreneur is everything to everybody. However, the lone ranger approach has its compensations. It reduces risks, permits quick decision making, and allows for correcting mistakes on a one-source basis. But no entrepreneur is an island (John Donne might have said) and a management team will have to be established down the line. The time will come when there are too many hats to wear and too many balls in the air. As the project becomes more complex, the taskload will signal time to bring management on board.

There are two schools of manning (personing?) thoughts. One advocates bringing on only management personnel adequately qualified for present job descriptions; a just-in-time (JIT) theory. The other suggests getting a team over-qualified in anticipation of growth. A questionable view is that over-qualified persons will do all pedestrian tasks better and slide into the complex future more smoothly.

The reasons against over-qualification are:

- Over-qualified persons are hard to find cost more, much more and are hard to convince.
- Over-qualified managers are less patient to hang in there. They may get a better offer and leave before the fat lady sings.
- Who knows what the future will bring? Changes occur and the management skills believed important may prove inappropriate.
- A time delay in the enterprise evolution can be costly with over-qualified and over-paid management.
- The wages have to be "pennies" today, but that is *de rigeur*. Startup life is a brown-bagger and not a three-martini lunch. The over-qualified may not wait.

On the balance, it makes more sense to staff with skills for today, not tomorrow. Caution: do not overstaff. It is not necessary to re-invent the corporation by filling every cubbyhole. The monthly servicing cost of overstaffing can be a hefty burden. Moreover, superfluous staff costs more than just salaries. Add-ons include benefits packages (equal to about 40% of salary), office space, taxes, telephones, secretaries, etc.

Liz Claiborne founded Liz Claiborne, a successful women's dress firm. She suggests,

> "Start with a low overhead and be willing to do everything yourself."

That may be an oversimplification, but it tells us that we should minimize our labor costs in the beginning.

Three or four can handle a startup: entrepreneur, financial person, and an "omnibudsperson" (all around handyperson). A little later will come the marketing person, and manufacturing specialist farther down the line.

Frequent dialogue and designated task assignments are vital to keep everyone up to speed. The entrepreneur must keep the team synergized, motivated, enthusiastic, and pumping in the same direction.

MIX THE GREEN PAINT

What Is The Bottom Dollar? The cost of money is a rationalizing factor. The first task is to calculate absolute dollars. The bankroll required is highly judgmental. That is all right, for the fundamental step is to think through how much will be needed to carry the firm through product development, market introduction, and profitability in three to five years.

Each new venture, bar none, is going to be cash intensive in every phase, seemingly feeding an alligator with an unsatiable appetite. To opt for too much money is an exercise in futility. It is a pipe dream to believe that investment money flows freely. Investors with fat wallets have sticky fingers. Getting it would give a false sense of security anyway. The debt servicing of large amounts of borrowed capital can be a bear. It is rare that an entrepreneur will get even what is wanted. On the other side, not enough money is a downer. It is a simple no-go! Consider that a short shrift may also be a sign of a lack of confidence in the project.

Here is a paradigm worth following:

Do not get too much money, if it is not necessary.
Do not get too little money, if it is necessary.

When any amount is promised, get it in writing! Do not plan on a one-lump-sum payment. It will never happen.

The following is an approximation:

There are many financing vehicles including pre-seed financing, bridge loans (small loans made prior to a finalized equity financing), public market purchases, secondary purchases, and compensating balance loans.

BEG, BORROW, OR STEAL?

The seed funding is the stage when the product is a glimmer, a reggae dream, and not a reality. It reaches for the pockets of the entrepreneur or

FINANCING STAGES

FINANCE	PRIMARY SOURCES	USE OF FUNDS	RANGE
Seed (To prove concept)	Personal Funds, Family, Friends Private investors Vendor Credit	Feasibility (Show How Money Will be Used)	$50K–$500K
1st Round (Startup)	Venture Capital Private Investors Partnerships Bank Lines of Credit Vendors	Product and Application (Beta Site Installation and Evaluation)	$300K–$5M
2nd Round (Expansion)	Venture Capital Private Investors Partnerships Customer Funding Vendor Participation	Implementation (Manufacturing and Marketing)	$2M–$10M
3rd Round (Rapid Growth)	Public Offering Capital Retained Earnings Debt Financing	Rapid Growth (Production and Marketing)	$10M–$50M

family. It is a very fragile and risky time, too dangerous for outside investors. If seed money could be generated from seed investors, it will cost an arm and a leg anyway. Digging into one's pocket is the only, if not the best, way to go.

WHEN WILL WE NEED THE MONEY?

Money is needed for garage R&D in addition to sweat capital. The overhead costs are minimal and the failure probability low. Once the product has been designed, is up and running or the concept has been established with some kind of beta testing, first round money may come for outside sources. In the second, third, and subsequent rounds of financing, the investment community takes part. At each round, additional pieces of the pie are traded away. As the new venture progresses, the giveaway pieces get smaller. Risk is perceived as inverse with each step up the ladder.

WHERE ARE THE DEEP POCKETS?

Personal Assets

Paul Levy of Rational refinanced his condominium to get going. Others have done likewise. Any liquid asset is worth money. A loan can be taken out on household furniture, family car, or you name it. What about the vacation home? It can be sold or refinanced.

Others have used personal savings accounts as collateral. Family jewels are good collateral. Working at another job might generate seed money. A dangerous ploy used has been to float credit cards. One entrepreneur reckoned that more than $100,000 can be borrowed with this vehicle, for a few months. In anticipation of an entrepreneurial try, an entrepreneur must not incur new personal debt. *Nyet* on the Betamax, PC, new car taking a Club Med vacation or buying clothes. This is commitment time and fiscal belt-tightening.

Family and Friends

Family and friends are the least likely to understand that any startup is highly speculative. They have faith in the entrepreneur which demands a deep personal responsibility. A response to delays or nonperformance will depend upon personal relationships. Therefore, one should not call upon family or friends who are not friendly. Never include family or friends as the last resort because "there is no alternative."

There are reasonable ways money can be obtained from family and friends:

- An unsecured loan at current bank rates with an option to acquire stock at a favorable price.
- A secured loan in a subordinated position; second or third.
- Stock sold at the seed level is usually less than $1 per share. Hopefully, the stock will go public in 2–4 years at 8 or 10 times seed investment.
- Family and friends may have strong financial statements. They might be willing to cosign on a loan for stock or options rights.

- A partnership might be formed to take advantage of tax shelter devices.

This is a time to check in with lawyers—those expensive legal eagles who are an absolute necessity in this litigious society.

Going short on legal fees makes no sense at all!

Banks

A good credit rating is square one. A previous banking relationship is a plus. Bankers work better with persons who have been customers of the bank for some time.

When the startup is anticipated, settle on one bank. Try to establish a relationship with one bank officer. A bank is a bank officer, in your case, not an organization. Aggregate all accounts in the bank which appear to look upon the venture or person with some favor. Those would be checking, savings, piggy bank, Christmas savings, money market, CDs; all accounts which are in banks. Do these things in advance, not at the moment.

Keep the friendly bank officer current on events taking place. Even if money is not needed, maintaining communications with the friendly banker is nurturing a valuable resource. Bankers are knowledgeable, free with financial advice, and it is often very helpful. Banks have a menu of money sources. They can refinance whatever assets the entrepreneur or family/friends have. They can provide a line of credit—secured or unsecured, make short term loans, they often have a few special investor customers.

Other Money Sources

There are private money baggers who have socked away money for investment opportunities: they can be tapped. It takes networking and talking with people, investment bankers, and entrepreneur groups to find out who they are. Remember that vendors are important sources. Some of them will put up funds, carry paper for a time, or float the material they provide. Be prepared to pay top dollar for supplies that are carried on the vendor's books. The pizza is never free. Vendor float is what Steve Jobs used effectively in the Apple startup. Frequently, new employees may be required to buy stock as a condition of employment. They might start with a split between a reduced salary and stock warrants. It can be an everyone wins situation. Dealing with venture capitalists requires a sophisticated and disciplined approach. Venture capitalist Ed Zschau notes that most of them have deep pockets and short arms! However, Rod Canion co-founded the very successful Compaq Computer startup. He said,

> "The best advice I ever received for starting a company was on how to pick a venture capital company.
>
> People think of venture capitalists as a source of money, which, of course, they are, but they can provide much more than money, and you should pick them carefully for the other things they can provide.
>
> In our case, we found a small partnership that was able to provide a lot of guidance, advice, and knowledge. They also opened doors to a lot of people in the financial industry."

How Much Do We Give Away?

It is a matter of negotiations in the trenches. There is no die cast format but an important mantra is:

> Never let an investment prospect get away.

One show stopper piece of advice is:

> "It is better to have 20% of something than 100% of nothing."

Here are some examples:

FUNDING TRADEOFFS

STAGE	RANGE	ENTREPRENEUR OWNERSHIP	INVESTOR OWNERSHIP
SEED	LOW —) (BOOTSTRAP)	100%	0%
	AVG — $50,000	80%	10%
	HIGH — $500,000	10%	80%
1st Round	L — $500,000	80%	15%
	A — $1,500,000	50%	50%
	H — $5,000,000	25%	75%
2nd Round	L — $2,000,000	80%	20%
	A — $4,000,000	65%	35%
	H — $10,000,000	40%	60%
3rd Round	L — $10,000,000	25%	80%
	A — $20,000,000	20%	85%
	H — $50,000,000	15%	90%

Legal Considerations

Make sure that legal counsel is sought, wisely and not expensively. Dr. Robert Collings, founder of Data Terminal Systems, uses attorneys but warns,

> "Never use lawyers to make business decisions; that's the CEO's job."

Cheap-fee lawyers are not the optimal choice. Obtain the best lawyer for the task and work out payment in advance. Lawyers will often trade services for stock interests.

Liabilities

Investors are gun-shy of potential liabilities and risk. This must be covered carefully. Also, the entrepreneur must investigate the future liabilities of any actions in which he and they are involved.

Legal Risks

Every startup is awash with legal trip bars. It is possible to get indentured for life on a personal basis. Officers and board members are legally liable and may be sued.

Under conditions of not withholding any federal taxes, the government may come after individual officers of the company, even if incorporated, and individual members of the Board as well. Shareholders and others may sue officers and board members. Indemnity insurance for board members and officers must be obtained. This issue is very important in the establishment of a new venture. The entrepreneur may have little risk but, when the entrepreneur or founders or board members have wealth, there are predator suers. The entrepreneur must be aware of legal potholes at every juncture. Examine every document, every commitment, and give deep consideration to the legal exposure of each option. Legal risk measurement calls for continuing surveillance. A legally protected enterprise reduces the probability of a calamity.

Tax Consequences

There are many investors foraging for tax shelters under new tax laws. But the days are gone when tax advantages are enough. The underlying premise must be a viable business with tax considerations as secondary issues.

It is important for the founders to structure the startup to minimize tax consequences if the firm goes public. Tax attorneys and tax accountants are essential specialists when dealing with tax consequences.

HOW CAN IT BE MADE TO WORK?

Develop the Product

Entrepreneurs must decide whether the product is designed to serve a supplier of current objects, components, or is a spanking new concept. An entrepreneur may invent a Cabbage Patch Doll II, a color screen for laptop computers, or avoidance radar for automobiles. Also, Tommy Davis, venture capitalist founder of the Mayfield Fund, said that he likes products which are not one-shot deals but can be sold over and over. The sagacious observation from that experienced entrepreneur is,

> "If you sell to the classes, you'll live with the masses. If you sell to the masses, you'll live with the classes."

As product planning and market selection are glued together, the first judgment of how the product will match the demand is harmonic convergence. Horizontally, it may be distributed through retail, product to user, or agents. This can be greased by knowing the consumer subgroup and understanding the product and buyer behavior. This may require an in-house sales staff. Vertically, the product may go to manufacturers, distributors, or other buffers between the product and the buyer. The vehicle of distribution is an extremely important decision.

It is given that the startup will be resource-limited. To develop more than one product or attempt to reach more than one market is to self destruct. Operating at more than one market level is "competing with customers." It is a conflict of interest, a deterioration of resources, and a double-whammy.

There are four key considerations to keep in mind:

1. The product can be an object, service, or whatever. The entrepreneur must not suffer from market myopia, to be hung up on the features of the product, and believe that the market will be waiting anxiously with open arms.

Lee Iacocca wrote about the Detroit syndrome of building a product (car) and then looking for a market. It did not work. It does not work. It will not work! That was changed at Chrysler. The market was determined first and then a car designed. It was a fine product with nuances included for market enticements.

The product features must be point-blank focused on a user group. Competition is a definite factor to be addressed in the development of a product. Consumers buy products to satisfy needs. The entrepreneur must know how the product is going to whip the butt off of the competition. Product orientation is not enough, it must be market-intensive.

2. The product is what it does. The customer buys a total package of benefits. Therefore, it is essential to design a product with functional utility. Thus, the product has a richer meaning than a simple object.

In a narrow sense, it may be physically undifferentiated. In a broader sense, the entrepreneur may differentiate the product significantly through quality, price, warranty, service, and/or reliability.

3. Products have different strokes for different folks. The entrepreneur must understand demographic variances in age groups, income categories, and geographic buying behavior, then develop a product which pinpoints demand accordingly.

4. The product must be adaptable. The product may have to adjust due to market behavior. In market theory, products are designed to serve specific demands. The market, as it changes, may require the product to alter its presumptive design.

Build A Prototype

Entrepreneurs build everywhere: dining rooms, bathrooms, bedrooms, workshops, kitchens, and even on the backs of station wagons. The point of building has little to do with the motivation, inspiration, or perspiration connected with a prototype.

Young Fred Gibbons had a garage startup with Software Publishing until the neighbors complained about the number of UPS trucks lined up in the driveway. He had to move.

Fred transferred to a formal facility in 1981. His firm went public in 1985 for $20,000,000. Sandra Kurtzig (ASK) had a kitchen-table startup.

Test It

Is the product ready for market? Many ventures tumble because the product is put on the market before its time. The numbers of untested products going to market are too many. Bill Bowman and David Seuss of Spinnaker Software visited retail outlets with their ideas of educational software. That market basket surveying altered the product they had in mind. Before they introduced it to market, they market tested their product again and again and again. It paid off in spades.

Fred Gibbons haunted trade shows armed with his software publishing concept. Firms in the business of selling software gave him some key suggestions and tips. It was back to the drawing board. When he developed his final prototype, he lugged it back to more trade shows for one last time. A few more recommendations later, he went into production.

Alvin Achenbaum wrote a book about the purpose of test marketing. He believes that the main value of testing is to learn about unsuspected problems and unforeseen opportunities.

Barbara Isaenberg started up the highly successful North American Bear, toys for children. She said,

> "My brother told me, 'If you don't like problem-solving, you shouldn't be in business, because everyday is filled with problems. You always think you'll never have a problem as bad as the last one you just solved, and the next day a bigger one comes along.'"

MARKETING

Market Development

The key is to understand the needs of the marketplace and to deliver the product or service more effectively than competitors. This is one-upmanship. That is value added. Thus, the entrepreneur calculates the level the market will be penetrated Gucci or K-Mart and does it better.

The product may:

1. Stimulate customers to purchase or increase their rate of purchase by utility, pricing, advertising, publicity, distribution, quality, and benefits.
2. Attract customers to buy it instead of competitor's.
3. Be geared to non-users or first time customers.
4. Open market segments not served.

Performance

The product must have a marketable appeal, cost or whatever. Or it must perform better at a higher price which buyers will be willing to pay. This squares with Harvard's Leavitt who refers to marketing as satisfying the needs of the buyer, while selling satisfies the needs of the seller.

Tactics

How the product is aligned and brought to the market requires careful planning and tactical implementation. How about distribution? Is it going to be in-house sales, catalog, distributor, retail, or wholesale? This must be carefully weighed, for it will affect tactical decision making.

Competition

It is unlikely that competitors will lie down and play dead if threatened. It is essential to estimate the competitive response prior to market entry. Competition serves most niches in markets. The trick is to enter market segments with a low profile and not arouse sleeping giants. Established competition usually has greater resources than the intruder. It is foolhardy to challenge an IBM even with an "unfair" advantage! An established and resource fat competitor can undersell, flood the market, and cream a new entrant with sheer dollar power!

American Airlines, reputedly with a billion dollars in its coffers, took on upstart People Express when People invaded American territory. American matched People fares and surrounded the People departure times. Within a year, People Express was reeling at the door of bankruptcy. American was out a few million dollars, a cheap shot to get rid of an invasive competitor. It was a red alert for other predators. Assume the market is an oligopoly, without competition. Will the customer still buy the product at the price? Is there a need? More importantly, a serviceable demand? There are external options that compete for disposable income. For example, would the customer buy a VCR instead of a weekend in Las Vegas? Once committed, it is "onward Christian soldiers marching as to war." The push is fast-forward, no veering side-to-side to reconsider, never looking behind to see what competition is doing.

Satchel Page said,

> "Don't ever look back 'cause they may be catching up on you."

In the matter of competition, an old saw is right on, "Offense is the best defense." Defensive competitive response is pure chicanery, counterproductive action.

Advertising and Promotion

The function of advertising and promotion is to get the message out to the market in the most effective way possible. This method requires one to:

- Define advertising goals quickly.
- Maximize consumer awareness and stimulate demand.
- Determine tasks to meet these objectives.
- Estimate cost/benefits of each choice.
- Know what the competition is doing, without following.

Determine The Market Position

Hundreds of superb technical inventions have faded into oblivion because of an ill-slated market position. The IBM Peanut, Tiny Tim, Edsel, Apple Lisa, and the new Coke, to name just a few. Build a better mousetrap and the world will not beat a path to your swinging door unless the world wants it.

In New York City, a publisher developed a product tailored for peoples' curiosity about the future.

The new periodical became the fastest-growing magazine in America (from 70,000 to 550,000 paid circulation in two years). No expensive premiums. No discounts. No gimmicks. It was a well-intended market position for the product.

UNDERSTAND THE PITFALLS, STUMBLES, AND FAILURES

A study by *Venture Economics*, with interviews, has shown that a typical venture capital portfolio will have the following return and experience over a 5–7 year period:

20% Bankruptcy ?–0X
40% Living Dead 0–1X
30% Good Returns 3–5X
10% Super Returns 5–100X

Pitfalls are moguls in the run which the entrepreneur must watch for incessantly. They are little traps into which an entrepreneur can fall unless handled correctly. Ego can be a pitfall. Tunnel thinking that there is only one way to do things is another. The list is long.

Stumbles are common in new ventures because of the unpredictability of the startup. New ventures are random and subject to a variety of uncontrollable forces. Perseverance and continuing the battle in the face of disappointments is SOP. Stumbles are not necessarily portenders of disaster. They are little problems that must be dealt with—and then press on.

If one entertains the notion that failure is failure, that is false. One pundit was the bearer of on-target tidings, though, when he wrote,

> "A *reasonable* new venture that does not reach its
> objectives and goals, may fail. But it is not a failure!
> It is a success for having tried."

Also, a project has not hit the failure mode until every avenue has been traveled and there is no other course.

Some Who Went For It

1. *Motivation.*   For four years, Donna Flaherty worked for a New England brokerage firm selling real estate, precious metals, oil, gas, and commodities. She got hooked on the natural resource industry.

Donna pulled up stakes and moved to Texas. She established contacts in the "oil patch" with two others, one with hands-on drilling experience and the other with selling experience in drilling packages.

Flaherty provided the management adhesive for the three. Her company is zooming. Why did Donna leave New England and security? Three trigger points: adventure, to know one's business inside out, and money.

2. *Mission.*   Sam Davis was a hungry entrepreneur. Every morning on his way to work the 28-year-old Chicago attorney looked for a place to pick up coffee and a muffin. He could not find the big fluffy muffins he used to get when he was studying law in Boston. Certain that the croissant craze had peaked, he envisioned a first-class muffin.

He studied muffins and became a high powered, committed muffin man. A banker loaned him $100,000. Newbury Muffins opened on busy Michigan Avenue. It has been busily ringing up spectacular sales. Franchising is now a viable option.

3. *Strategy.*   Ray Williams started a part-time painting job. It was painting oil tanks on weekends for $100 each. Business calls kept ringing the phone off the hook. In three years he quit his job as an insurance adjuster. He started small, bootstrapping, and scrambled to keep his head above water. Business blossomed. He built up his inventory, set up a distribution network, advertised products, and booked orders, according to his strategy. Business was excellent and growth rapid. Then he ran headlong into a textbook case of a cashflow crunch. He nearly closed the doors because he almost ran out of money. But he hung in there.

From the feedback experience, he is doing a better job of managing cash to growth. He is on target now. Ray's Tank Services, Inc. will do about $4-million this year. There was a chain reaction, and Ray now has six related services which he sells.

His well-calculated strategy calls for earning a 40% return compounded annually over five to seven years.

4. *Mobility.*   Clayton Jones is the 62-year-old founder of Fiesta Salons in Columbus, Ohio. Clayton is successful though he has stumbled many, many times. The perpetual-motion Clayton Jones says,

> "Formula for failure: try 32 times. Formula for
> success: try 33 times."

5. *Passion.*   Sally Tassani's firm handles $10 million in advertising and marketing a year. She is seven years into her business—seven years of six days a week, fourteen-plus hours a day. Why?

> "I suppose I could boil it down to one word and
> that would be passion."

Passionate in business accurately describes Sally Tassani.

6. *Tenacity.*   Eric Pietz is in his thirties and last year revenues of his Financial Communications, Inc. topped $1-million. He says:

> "It's tenacity more than anything else that leads to success."

Mary Kay Ash looks at tenacity as persistence and determination.

7. *Sensibility.*   Liz Claiborne simply believes women should have the kind of clothes that will match their working lifestyle. Her sensible, but strongly-felt idea grew into the multimillion-dollar Liz Claiborne, Inc.

8. *Accomplishment.*   Milton Maltz, Malrite Communications Group, started as a child actor on Chicago radio. He bought a rural radio station in Wisconsin and turned it into the Dairy Farmer's Station. He began to buy more and more radio stations.

He now controls 17 stations, and his stock is worth more than $8 million. The IPO (Initial Public Offering) did not change his lifestyle. Milt says,

> "I didn't go public so I could enjoy the good life. The good life is running the company and watching it grow."

9. *Experience.*   Vincent Coates is not a new millionaire. He has been one for years, the result of experience in many startups.

Vincent's latest startup is Nanometrics, Inc. The company makes electron microscopes. Coates says,

> "I feel the urgency to get organized."

That is particularly true since he has gone public. He kept all of his $41.9 million in stock because he believed the price was too low. It will not be long before Coates will experience another startup.

Fred Gibbons of Software Publishing identifies experience as a requisite for successful entrepreneuring. He put in four years at Hewlett-Packard before launching his software company.

Dr. Srully Blotnick agrees that experience is valuable, particularly in high technology. Dr. Blotnick wrote,

> "Those over 35 have worked for a while, have more exposure, can use their knowledge to husband their money, and are more likely to make a success of their new venture."

10. *Vindication.* Charles Scharfe took his Comstock Group public last year, and his stock was worth about $22 million. He had a great feeling of "vindication and victory." He tried to take the firm public in 1978, and it failed. A merger went sour. He was burned by an antitrust suit and was driven to vindicate himself. Charles made it. He also found that it was easy to get bank financing after going public successfully. It also put a value on his holdings and afforded easy liquidity.

SOME COMMON MYTHS

1. Disappointments do not have to be.
2. Wait for the right time to start.
3. Money is more important than accomplishment.
4. Settle only for the total bundle up front.
5. Work, work, work; no play, play, play.
6. People will work less unless they are watched.
7. Risk can be eliminated.
8. Mistakes are examples of poor judgment.
9. Plan carefully and it will turn out that way.
10. Giving up may be the best thing.

UNCOMMON TRUTHS

1. It will happen only if you make it happen.
2. Focus and know your business.
3. Attitude will affect altitude.
4. Friends, relatives, and business do not mix.
5. A startup is no piece of cake, never was and never will be.

6. Sneak into markets quietly with no hoopla.
7. With capital, you can be a roaring success, without it, you are on hold.
8. In every crisis there is opportunity.
9. A 50-50 deal is no deal at all.
10. To succeed unethically is not to succeed at all.
11. Temper gets us into trouble, pride keeps us there.

10
THE BOTTOM LINE

THE GREAT BEYOND

Let the words of Buckminster Fuller ring in your ears,

> "Look out in the universe for something that
> needs to be done and do it!"

ACCOMPLISHMENT

In the past 50 years we have made massive strides toward comfort—learning to manage heating and air conditioning and finding ways to control pain. The daily drudgeries are being dealt with by machines, computers, and robots. We play games on television sets; the direction of society has been to turn inward. We have made giant steps in developing thinking computers. Then there are laser beams, biotechnology, cellular technology, fax machines, visual telephones, and a multitude of advancements to affect our lives. Much of this has been good, but it has also created a misconception that the purpose of life is self-nurturing, to attain a blissful state of nirvana with no struggle, sacrifice, discomfort, strain, or pain. The ethos of entitlement is ingrained and pervasive, and its effect on the quality of life has been enormous.

In the U.S., the focus of efforts is on consumption and not production short term hedonism instead of long term accomplishment. We strive for the quick fix of immediate gratification, often without the pathos of effort.

Other countries, particularly the Pacific Rim countries of Asia, are producers instead of consumers, and they are forging ahead in the world markets. It does not have to be bad for those who are willing to be creative and inventive willing to work hard. The opportunities for those who opt to swing out of the self-serving environment are enormous. For life just does not work that way.

Ben Franklin said, "There's no gain without pain." It is as true today as it was when it appeared in *Poor Richard's Almanac*. The orbiting goals of becoming what one is capable of becoming can be achieved by those who are willing to pay the price of commitment and suffer the sweet pain of perseverance. That is the way of the entrepreneur: dedication, sacrifice, discomfort, strain, pain, and gain. Having climbed that mountain, the entrepreneur will enjoy the rich aphrodisiac of accomplishment. It is a vintage joy rarely experienced.

Life Enrichment

Over and over, entrepreneurs have found that life has become sweet as cherry pie after a successful startup. The fulfillment can be overwhelming. In addition to having captured the brass ring in a new venture, money flows freely to make life bountiful and beautiful for those who know how to spend it.

Family Benefits

During a startup, the entire family takes on the burden and sacrifices. The entrepreneur has had to devote his days and nights and weekends to the new venture. Dinner table conservation is almost always absorbed with daily knotty startup problems and the children are often ignored. After all, the entrepreneur is engaged in a life and death struggle! When the new venture finally goes public and the entrepreneur has harvested, it is show-

and-tell time for the family. Though the entrepreneur will probably be limited in stock sales of treasury stock to a small percentage each year, it will be enough for the good life.

Social Good

A successful startup satisfies a consumer demand in a way that is most efficient and effective. In that sense, a new venture improves the quality of life. In addition, a profitable enterprise adds to the community by providing jobs for people. A new firm pays into the tax coffers of the City, State, and Federal Government. Also, a successful venture adds to the dignity of the community by giving it pride and substance.

When A Growing Company Is A Grown Company

Taking companies into the public offering market is one of three ways to recoup an investment. The second way is for a startup company to be acquired by another. The third way, not often followed, is to ride with the new venture all of the way to maturity as a private company.

How Now Cash Cow?

In the startup phase, Cash Flow is the Crown Prince. It is a cash-intensive time. As the firm passes through the rapid growth stage, it may develop into a Cash Cow, throwing off considerable money on a regular basis. When a startup becomes a Cash Cow, it is an appropriate time to determine what the strategy will be to protect that position. Typically, 10—20% of revenue should go into research to upgrade the product or service to keep that leading edge honed.

Perhaps 8–10% should be put into reserves for depreciation of equipment and replacement costs.

The most successful companies in the United States have proven to be those which reduce their debt to achieve the lowest possible debt-to-equity. A Cash Cow is in a highly bucolic state; it is enticingly vulnerable. Competition lurks in the wings like vultures, ready to challenge and snatch the lead. This is a particularly dangerous time. Resting on laurels can court disaster. The strategy must be aggressiveness for a positive cash flow which can only be protected by re-investing, by conservative actions, and with well-thought-out cash-flow strategies.

Where Did The Challenge Go?

After the product or service has penetrated the market, professionalism in management becomes much more needed than gut feel and spontaneous decision-making. Following market introduction, it is not unusual for the entrepreneur to feel that the challenge has frittered away and the fun is gone. When the entrepreneur harbors that feeling, it is time to harvest, pull stakes, and move on.

An Entrepreneur As Manager Rarely Works

In this chaotic throws of starting up, the instinctive and intuitive rapid fire manager functions well as a gunslinger. When the firm reaches rapid growth and levels of stability, experienced management is the call, with skills alien to those of an entrepreneur. It is simply a factoid, as Norman Mailer calls an inaccuracy, that entrepreneurs work just as well in rapid growth and mature stages, for entrepreneurs as managers are about as compatible as oil and water. To paraphrase Greyhound, professional managers say that entrepreneurs "should leave the managing to us."

These Ways Out With Rose Petals

More than 40,000 businesses change hands every year and about 80% of the owners do not achieve the full profit potential because they made one or more common bloopers.

The entrepreneur seller should be wary, for a business is sold once in a lifetime, from an entrepreneur's perspective, while the ratio of buyers is about six to one.

The typical corporate acquirer or leveraged buyout expert will scoop up seven companies or more in a two-year period. The average private buyer will buy about five. The entrepreneur, for sake of simplicity, will sell one in ten years or a lifetime. The entrepreneur is a babe in the woods, by comparison.

When negotiating with a corporate buyer or leveraged buyout group or a sophisticated private buyer, there is a specific methodology for optimization:

1. Position the company for sale.

   The time to sell out may not be when the seller wants to sell but when it is right for the buyer.
   Try not to sell at the low end of the season or when the market is down or before the product has reached the market.
   In the midst of an aggressive, upbeat sales program, a surge of positive publicity, business on the upswing; those are the best times for selling and reaping the harvest rewards.

2. Value of the business.

   Many sellers do not know how to determine the true value of their business.
   Financial statements are often prepared for the IRS, shareholders, or some other entity and may not reflect the true value of the business. Good will, debts, and real market value of assets are important considerations and must be valued correctly.

3. Unrealistic price.

   After determining the true value of the business, the worth to the seller is important but only as information.
   The price must be in the ballpark of the true value, not what the seller hopes to get.
   The realistic price of the business is what a buyer is willing to pay and a seller is willing to sell, nothing more or less.

4. Analyze the buyers.

   An appraisal of the buying firm is necessary.
   Determine if they have the ability to perform, the assets they indicated, the reserves to carry out the contractual agreement, and the experience necessary to finalize the deal.

Buyers have been known to inflate their statements. Some knowingly give our erroneous information. It is necessary to check them out!

5. Understand the buyer's motives.

   In selling, dwell on those issues which appeal to the buyer.
   Buyers generally are looking for return on investment and growth potential.
   Pride of ownership, seller's sweat and equity, and societal motivations are all of relatively little interest to the buyers.

6. Sell to the right group.

   It may be wise to sell the firm to a qualified company or group who can guarantee the future viability of the enterprise.
   Too often, sellers take the highest price, forsaking the best fit. They end up getting back a decimated company in foreclosure. Be careful of the buying group. If it is a long-term payout, are you certain they can meet their commitments?

7. Get professional help.

   Use an intermediary, a professional.
   It is too easy to get bad advice.
   Investment houses have sophisticated and capable teams with selling and negotiating skills.

8. Have proper documentation and legal procedures.

   This is one of the reasons for using professionals.
   Legal advice is crucial. Do not leave home without it.
   The form of the sale, the vehicle, is extremely important and may have a significant influence on the outcome.
   A buying group will be apprehensive if documentation is inadequate or procedures foundered.
   Moreover, given legal costs and the cost of time, it is prudent to make certain that documentation is proper so there is not a comeback at a later day. Though it may be costly to adhere to the proper legal form, in the end it is financially beneficial.

REASONS IT ALL MAKES SENSE

Finally, the process is this. Fear, apprehension, and willingness to venture is the entrance fee. Willing to work your buns off is the row to hoe. Success is the first prize, the blue ribbon. Selling out and walking away is a lovely amble at the end of the rainbow. It takes guts and conviction to become an entrepreneur. One has to summon courage and cut the safety lines. It takes perseverance and persistence. The hours may be long and hard. Crises are the standard daily fare. All have to be juggled as if they are lighted torches.

Success is a fitting reward for the person who has gone the distance. After harvesting and leaving, the road ahead becomes smoother and the chaotic pace slows to a shuffle. It is not the finish line, it is the first lap for a better life.

SUMMARY

In summary, anyone can become an entrepreneur. That is a snap. There are no limiting factors to dreaming. The entrepreneur must have a magnificent obsession and vision. It is the becoming that does demand action and commitment. It requires planning and doing. Luck and timing will play a heavy hand. The entrepreneur must be prepared for a passel of mistakes and goofs and disappointments. Yet the road to successful entrepreneurship is a fun time. It may not seem so during the launching of the enterprise but it is invigorating and stimulating. Next to remember is that ethics and truth are demanded in a new venture. Short-sheeting the investors or one's self will lead to rack and ruin.

Most important, never, never, never, never, never, never, give up!

AUTHOR INDEX

SUBJECT INDEX